# THE HUMAN ANIMAL

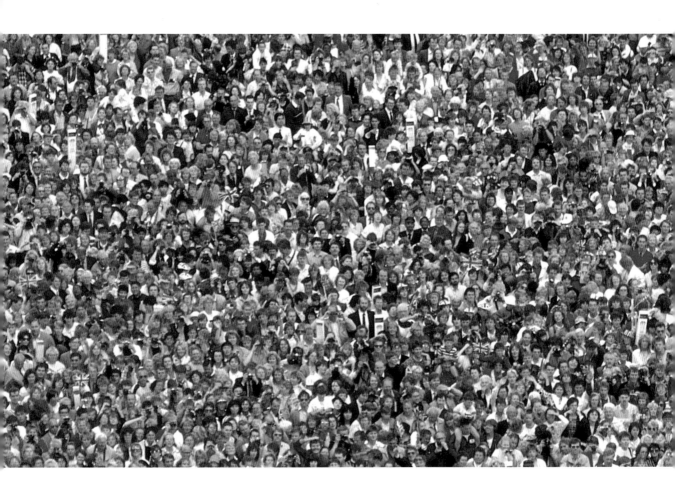

# THE HUMAN ANIMAL

*A Personal View of the Human Species*

## DESMOND MORRIS

**BCA**

LONDON    NEW YORK    SYDNEY    TORONTO

This book is published to accompany the
television series entitled *The Human Animal*
which was first broadcast in June 1994
This edition published 1994 by
BCA by arrangement with BBC Books
a division of BBC Enterprises Limited,
Woodlands, 80 Wood Lane
London W12 0TT

First published 1994
© Desmond Morris 1994
CN 2306

Designed by Harry Green

Set in Garamond Simoncini
by Selwood Systems, Midsomer Norton
Printed and bound in Great Britain
by Butler & Tanner Ltd, Frome
Colour separation by Radstock
Reproductions, Midsomer Norton
Jacket printed by Lawrence Allen Ltd,
Weston-super-Mare

# Contents

# *Introduction*

Human beings are animals. We are sometimes monsters, sometimes magnificent, but always animals. We may prefer to think of ourselves as fallen angels but in reality we are risen apes.

Everything we do has an inborn, genetic basis and all our activities have something in common with other species. Uniquely, however, we have built on these animal patterns, exaggerating and elaborating them to an amazing degree and sometimes suppressing them with damaging consequences.

The cultural variations on our biological themes have often been so dramatic and so impressive that they have obscured the underlying similarity of all mankind. This has often led to disastrous and unnecessary conflict and destruction. We have behaved as though each of our societies belonged to a different species, in deadly competition one with another.

In the past many studies of human behaviour have focussed on our local customs and traditions and their countless, varying details. They have stressed our superficial differences and, in the process, have ignored our more fundamental similarities. What is needed now is a biological portrait of our species, to redress the balance.

Despite the many fascinating variations that exist from region to region and society to society, every one of the thousands of millions of human beings alive today shares an almost identical genetic inheritance. We may wear different hats but we all show the same smile; we may speak different languages but they are all rooted in the same basic grammar; we may have different marriage customs but we all fall in love. Despite our different skin colours, religious beliefs and social rituals, we are biologically astonishingly close to one another.

If you doubt the truth of such a statement, consider this: it is now known that we share 98.4 per cent of our genetic make-up with the chimpanzee. If our genes only differ by 1.6 per cent from those of the speechless, shuffling, hairy ape that we have looked down upon for so many years, then how much can we humans differ, one from another?

To take this a little further, recent studies in molecular biology have proved that the gorilla and the orang-utan are more distantly related to the chimpanzee than we are. Not so long ago a major distinction was made between us, the humans, on the one hand and them, the great apes, on the other. The divide was thought to be enormous, so much so that when, back in 1967, I had the audacity to write a book in which I referred to our species as 'The Naked Ape', I was widely accused not only of assaulting human dignity but also of distorting evolution.

Anthropologists attacked me, saying it was ludicrous to refer to man as an ape; that even to suggest such a close relationship was a gross misrepresentation of our family tree. They favoured the idea of a much more remote separation of our ancestors from the rest of the primates, with the human line splitting off at a very early stage. A quarter of a century later they are strangely quiet about these criticisms. Even anthropologists, it now appears, were suffering from the age-old indoctrination that drums into us the false idea that man is somehow separate from the other animals, rather than an integral part of nature.

We owe far more to our animal inheritance than we are usually prepared to admit. But instead of being ashamed of our animal nature, we can view it with respect. If we understand it and accept it, we can actually make it work for us. If we try to deny it, suppress it or distort it, we are in danger of building a tension, both in ourselves and in our societies, that will eventually explode. This could even destroy us as a species if we ignore it too long.

As a zoologist I try to bring an objective approach to the study of mankind. I attempt to see our species as just another life-form and to avoid the usual prides and prejudices about the way we conduct our lives. My method, like that of any other field-naturalist, is that of the observer. I am a watcher rather than an experimenter. I use my trained eye to see, as clearly as possible, the patterns of human activity. Hence the title of this book: *The Human Animal*.

If I succeed, I will lead you into the very centre of the human arena as an invisible witness, able to watch the events unfold there as if seeing them for the first time. The most ordinary and commonplace will, I hope, be revealed as subtle and fascinating; the most bizarre and obscure as suddenly understandable.

# 1
# *The Language of the Body*

The Earth is a small, friendly planet that was formed about four and a half thousand million years ago. For the past six hundred million years its surface has been cool enough to support a huge variety of life-forms. It has seen the evolution of over a million species of animals and nearly half a million species of plants, each competing for a small slice of the action.

Recently, however, one species of animal has come to dominate all other life-forms and to alter dramatically the face of the Earth. A puny primate, with no natural weapons – no venom, no sharp spines, no fangs or claws – its success story is remarkable. Presumptuously self-named *Homo sapiens* – the Wise Man – this strange little ape gave up its old way of life, stood up on its hind legs and started to talk. Then, equipped with little more than an enlarged brain, this compulsively curious, constantly chattering creature began to stride out across the surface of the globe, taking all before it. The rest of the story is, quite literally, history.

Today there are more than five thousand million human beings teeming all over the land mass, taming it and moulding it. Every twenty-four hours another quarter of a million people are added to the world population. This is a species we need to understand if we are to survive. What makes this amazing animal tick? What is the secret of its lavish, unprecedented success?

In my zoological career, before I turned to the subject of human beings, I had studied the behaviour of many different kinds of fish, birds and mammals. With those, I could not carry on a conversation. I was forced to learn simply by watching their actions. It occurred to me to use the same method when investigating human behaviour. Instead of listening to what people said, I would observe what they did. I would observe them in their natural habitats, like a bird-watcher. I would become a manwatcher.

This approach was very different from the lengthy verbal sessions of psychoanalysts, the precise questionnaires of sociologists, the laboratory tests of psychologists or the tribal interrogations of anthropologists. It involved travel to over sixty countries. It meant attending every conceivable kind of human event, from riots to royal garden parties, from sumo to opera, from carnivals to cremations, from political rallies to camel markets, from pop concerts to cup finals. Above all, it meant watching people in their most ordinary, everyday environments, in the streets and shops, the parks and offices, the gardens and the countryside.

The quest was to find out how people really behaved, without intruding on their lives, in order to obtain an undistorted view of their conduct. The moment an anthropologist starts interviewing a tribesman he automatically alters that person's behaviour; he has become a part of it himself. All too often this has meant that the tribesmen in question have told him what they think he wants to hear, rather than the truth about their society. In a similar way, when human 'subjects' enter a psychologist's laboratory, they are immediately on their guard. Their behaviour tightens up and becomes more considered and forced. Only if they are left alone in their normal world do people behave in a spontaneous and natural manner. And if the occasion does become more formal, then the formality in their actions is directed, not at the scientist, but at the event itself.

My first task was to make what is called an 'ethogram' of human actions. An ethogram is a list of every characteristic movement or posture made by the members of a particular species. With a fish or a bird the list is long. With humans it is immense. I spent several years assembling hundreds of files of photographs of every possible kind of gesture, gesticulation, facial expression, body posture, limb action and form of locomotion. I started to classify them and to work out the many local variations that exist as one moves from region to region around the globe.

I soon began to notice that there were different types and categories of actions, and found, to my surprise, that people were far more predictable than I had imagined. This upset me slightly because, like most adults, I cherish the fantasy of being unpredictable since unpredictability implies personal freedom – something which most people today value highly. If, when closely observed, we turn out to be all too predictable, this suggests an almost robotic existence, an idea we find distasteful.

The truth, however, is that with our human body language we are all creatures of habit. Unless we are drunk, drugged or temporarily insane, we stick to a remarkably fixed set of personal body actions that are as typical of each of us as our fingerprints. Whether we are smiling, shaking a fist, wiping our nose or putting on our shoes, we nearly always perform the movements in the same way every time. It takes an immense amount of effort for a great actor to adopt a body language that is entirely alien to his own. Most of us never try. And we would be hopeless at it if we did. For each of us, our body language is like a signature.

So what exactly are the elements of this visual language of the body? The most extraordinary thing we do, as animals, is so familiar that we take it completely for granted: walking. Unlike any other mammal, we walk about all day long on our hind legs. Some other species may hop along on their hind legs and a few, like bears and gibbons, occasionally rear up and waddle clumsily forward but we are the only true mammalian bipedal walkers.

Amazingly, specialists are still arguing over why we took this strange, vertical step during the course of our evolution. One idea comes from watching our closest living relatives, the chimpanzees. If they find themselves faced with the unusual task of having to carry too much food, they are forced to adopt a clumsy, vertical posture. When our ancient human ancestors first turned to hunting as a way of life, they must have faced the tricky problem of how to carry home the bacon. On all fours this would have been almost impossible and, to start with, the kill was probably consumed on the spot. But if the meat was to be brought back to the safety of the home base, where it could be shared with the rest of the group, then carrying must have become a regular human chore.

In a similar way, female food-gathering could have been improved by the simple invention of a container – a primitive bag or basket of some sort – which would have permitted the collecting and carrying home of large numbers of vegetable foods, such as berries, nuts, fruits and roots.

A second idea sees the act of carrying as a later development. Our ancestors, it is argued, originally took to standing upright as a way of seeing over long grasses and peering into the distance. This would have given them a considerable advantage when searching for prey or keeping a look-out for predators. Or it could have been used merely to satisfy their curiosity. Today, grass monkeys in Africa can occasionally be seen to rear up in this way, when they are alarmed or inquisitive, although they always return to a four-footed posture

*Our ability to move about freely on our hind legs is so familiar to us that we take it for granted, but it is one of the most important features of the human species. It freed our hands and turned us, literally, into the most manipulative animal on earth. By comparison, other apes are clumsy when they try to stand up straight.*

before moving off. This argument might explain standing up but the more difficult task of walking along bipedally is another matter.

The latest explanation of our unique body posture is based on tests with four-legged and two-legged models of early ape-men. With a simulated sun overhead it was found that the 'quadruped' human model was much more exposed to overheating. Computer calculations revealed that, by standing up, we reduced by sixty per cent the amount of heat beating down on our bodies from the blazing African sun. Retaining a thick covering of long head hair protected just those parts directly exposed to the sun's rays – the top of the head and shoulders. In addition, by raising most of the human body up away from the baking earth, we gained further benefits from any slight breezes there might have been. The combined result was a vitally important improvement in body cooling, a modification that gave us a huge advantage over other predators. Being quadrupeds, they were forced to avoid overheating on the chase by favouring the hours of darkness. With our new, cooling posture, we could hunt even in the heat of the day.

Whichever theory is correct, as soon as we stood tall as a species, several things happened. We viewed one another in a totally new way. What had been the discreetly hidden under-belly now became the full frontal display. We found ourselves facing one another with our genitals exposed. We also found it difficult to defecate without soiling ourselves and one of the first tasks for our newly liberated hands must have been to invent the primeval equivalent of toilet paper.

Our front feet, now our nimble hands, had many other duties. We could make tools, build huts and start to modify our environment in an entirely novel way. In a million years we progressed from flint axes to space rockets, the whole of modern technology being initiated by the simple act of standing up on our hind legs.

Our front feet also became incredibly expressive. When other animals become emotionally excited, they sometimes paw the ground with a hoof or stamp the earth in anger, alarm or frustration. That is all. But we, at a rough estimate, make at least three thousand different gestures using our hands and fingers … and that does not include the highly specialized hand sign-language employed by the deaf.

Each one of us uses our hands as signalling devices every day of our lives. Many of these signals are made unconsciously as we talk, our hands beating time, like the batons of orchestra conductors, to our spoken words. These 'baton gestures' help to emphasize our words but they also convey our changing moods. The precise posture of the hand as it beats the air tells us something about the emotional state of the speaker.

One of the best locations to study this type of gesture is a political rally. Each speaker has already worked out his verbal message, usually a string of highly predictable platitudes calculated to gain him applause. But while he is mouthing these utterances, his hands are also busy. He will not be aware of precisely what they are doing, merely that they are beating time to his statements and helping to underline them. If we ignore his words and focus exclusively on his hands, it soon becomes clear that he employs eleven major hand signals.

If he is making a powerful point, he will clench his fist, as if about to punch an invisible opponent. If he is trying to chop down a rival proposal, he switches instead to the hand-chop gesture, cutting down through the air as forcibly as possible with a flattened hand, its hard edge pointing down. With this action he transforms his hand into a symbolic axe.

For those who wish to appear forceful, but not too violent, there is a slightly milder hand posture – the semi-clenched fist. In this, the hand makes a limp fist but without curling the thumb around the knuckles. With the thumb uppermost, on top of the bent forefinger, this half-fist is jerked in the air to emphasize point after point in the speaker's words. It is almost as if he is serving an invisible writ on his audience. This gesture is favoured by politicians who, although cautious, are nonetheless determined to push their policies through.

If the politician is making a more precise point, he will abandon these power gestures and use a more delicate finger action. As his words arrive at the moment of precision, his thumb and forefinger come together, as if holding something very small with great care.

In a more dominant mood, the speaker introduces the palm-down hand posture, usually with a few slight downward movements. In this he is symbolically calming down his audience, as if it were composed entirely of unruly children. If he is less sure of himself, he uses the opposite hand signal, with the palm up. This is the imploring gesture of the beggar, reaching out his hand for help. This particular gesture is universal and can even be seen in wild chimpanzees when begging for food from companions.

A special variation of the palm-up posture is the hand shrug in which the fingers are

*When we become emotional, we make movements with our hands that reflect our changing moods. We may use a power grip, beating a fist to emphasize a strong point (above left), or employ a delicate precision grip to make a fine point (above right). We may use a wagged forefinger as a symbolic club to beat people over the head (below left), or a stabbed forefinger like a dagger, to thrust home a point (below right).*

*The position of our palms as we speak may implore (above left), repel (above right), reach out to (below left) or embrace our audience (below right).*

slightly curled. The curl increases more and more from the forefinger to the little finger, creating a hand shape that looks as though the speaker is holding a large, invisible ball in each hand. This is the unconscious disclaimer gesture and usually signifies either a protestation of innocence or deceit.

If the speaker wishes his audience to embrace his ideas, he offers them a hint of an embrace in his hand gestures. He reaches out both hands, with the palms facing one another, as if trying to hug his audience at a distance. This is a favourite gesture of good communicators, who know the value of making their audience feel intimate with those on the platform. A variation of it involves curving the arms around, so that the speaker's palms face his own body. This palm-back gesture is a symbolic embrace. He holds the air in front of his body as if it contains each member of his audience, hugged to his chest.

Finally, there are two special forefinger gestures much loved by the more aggressive politicians. One is the prodding forefinger, aimed straight towards the audience, as if stabbing them into submission. The other is the wagging forefinger. In this the stiff finger is raised vertically and then brought down like a miniature club on an imagined head. Beating the finger in the air in this way is favoured by many a domineering speaker, unaware perhaps that the audience will find it a patronizing, headmasterish gesture.

There are, of course, many other gesticulations employed during speech-making but these eleven are the firm favourites. Because both the speaker and the audience are primarily focussed on the words being spoken, none of these gestures is deliberately made or deliberately read. They form a sub-text which carries with it a mood communication system that imparts far more information than any of those present may realize. They will transmit to the audience either a feeling that the speaker is not to be trusted or that he means what he says. If his verbal message is false or exaggerated, his gestures will give him away. They will make a 'bad fit' with his words and leave the audience uncomfortable, without knowing quite why. If they match well with the spoken words, the listeners will unconsciously sense that harmony and will respond more positively.

All these gesticulations have been made possible by the vertical posture of our species, releasing our front feet from the task of locomotion. Another benefit of this shift is the much more precise ability we have to indicate direction to our companions. This may seem a trivial action but in our earlier days it must have been of immense value on the hunt. When wolves hunt they can only indicate the direction of the prey by pointing their whole body towards it. We see this clearly today in the hunting dogs called pointers, which freeze and stiffly aim themselves in the direction of a new scent they have just picked up.

For humans, such body pointing would be a crudely inefficient way of indicating direction. Early tribesmen used instead the stiff forefinger. They signalled direction by the horizontal angle of the finger and distance by the vertical angle. The higher the forefinger was tilted, the further away was the object. It was as if the finger was a symbolic arrow or spear, to be fired through the air at a distant target. The more remote the target, the higher the weapon would have to be aimed.

To find today's most colourful human pointers, we have to travel to the lands of the Mediterranean region. There, where the point-duty policeman has managed to survive the introduction of traffic lights, it is possible to witness a series of directional gestures that any orchestra conductor would envy. The arms flail, the fingers jab the air, the hands flourish, the chin juts and the whole body quivers stiffly on the police podium. This is a dying art, increasingly swept away by modern technology, to our loss.

While our hands are gesticulating, our faces are grimacing. Anatomically, we have the most expressive faces in the entire animal kingdom. At the other end of the scale is a creature such as the crocodile. This has only four facial expressions: mouth and eyes open, mouth and eyes shut, mouth open with eyes shut and mouth shut with eyes open – not exactly an expressive range to test a great actor.

The problem for the crocodile is that its entire facial region is encased in heavy armour and completely rigid. Moving up the expressive scale to the typical monkey, the facial region becomes much more flexible. The skin that covers the head can be moved slightly. By stretching or relaxing it, the animal can raise and lower its forehead. With special colour patches backing up these small movements, flashing brow signals can be made. It can frown or stare. Also, the hair on top of its head can be flattened or made to stand on end.

Around the monkey's mouth are muscular lips that can be pouted, pulled back or curled into a snarl. The tongue can be flapped or waggled. This is now a highly expressive face, capable of transmitting a whole variety of emotional signals. There are slight variations from species to species, but basically all monkeys use the same face-language.

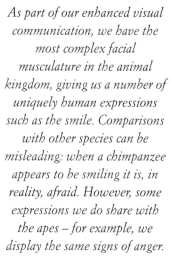

As part of our enhanced visual communication, we have the most complex facial musculature in the animal kingdom, giving us a number of uniquely human expressions such as the smile. Comparisons with other species can be misleading: when a chimpanzee appears to be smiling it is, in reality, afraid. However, some expressions we do share with the apes – for example, we display the same signs of anger.

No animal in the world has a more expressive face than the human being, although our nearest living relative, the chimpanzee, comes close.

The most primitive theme in monkey expressions is the one that deals with aggression and runs from extreme hostility to extreme fear. As a general rule, it can be said that the more hostile a monkey is feeling, the more its head skin is pulled forward. If its mood changes and it becomes more and more frightened, the skin is pulled back further and further. It is as if, in the heat of the moment, the head skin itself is trying to advance or retreat.

The effect of these skin shifts is to make an aggressive monkey lower its brows into a staring frown, while a scared animal raises its eyebrows to the maximum. If there is a crest of hair on top of the head, the forward movement of the head skin results in the crest being erected, making the animal look suddenly bigger. If the monkey is scared, the crest will fall back flat on the skull, making it look smaller.

Around the monkey's mouth the same sort of skin shift takes place. Angry lips are brought forward, while frightened lips are pulled back. Because, during aggressive encounters, the jaws are slightly open, ready to bite if necessary, the lip movements expose the teeth in a special way. The angry monkey exposes only its front teeth, while the scared one shows them all.

We humans share these expressions with our monkey relatives. Our eyebrows are lowered into a fierce frown when we are angry and arched upwards during moments of panic. We may not boast an erectile crest of hair on top of our heads but even without that particular adornment we are able to show a slight rise or fall in the hairline. And our adult males do have the special compensation of a dramatic beard that they can jut forward aggressively in close encounters of the hostile kind.

Also, our lips closely follow the monkey pattern during disputes. We pull them open vertically in a vicious snarl when we are ready to attack, showing only our incisors and canines. In this highly hostile mood our mouth corners are brought forward, concealing our molars. If, by contrast, we are intensely frightened, our mouth corners are fully retracted, exposing all our molar teeth in an expression of abject fear.

In these respects we reveal our close ties with our primate relatives. But we go far beyond them in the subtlety of our expressions and in their variety. We have a whole range of uniquely human facial signals, from the cocked eyebrow and the wrinkled nose to the wink and the smile.

Smiling is perhaps our most important facial expression. We have added to the monkey back-and-forth lip movements an up-and-down variation all of our own. By turning our mouth corners up, we can signal happiness and by turning them down we can convey sadness. And by using the 'happy mouth' as a greeting we can convey instant friendliness.

This may sound obvious but it was vitally important for us to evolve such an expression. As a hunting species, in primeval times, we had to become increasingly cooperative if we were to survive. And we needed a quick and easy way of signalling our friendly feelings to one another. The smile was the perfect answer. Other primates do have friendly signals, such as lip smacking and teeth chattering, but those are not so easy to perform or so visible at a distance. The great human grin can be seen from far away and, if necessary, the cheerful smile can be flashed on and off in a split second. It can also be held for some time without difficulty and can be varied in many subtle ways to suggest differing degrees of friendship or love.

In childhood the smile is especially important. Our human infants, having no maternal fur to cling to, must find some other way of ensuring that they stay close to the all-protective mother. The smile arrives early, in about the fourth week of life, and it enchants the mother. If her baby smiles up at her she automatically wants to cuddle it, or at least stay close to it. In maintaining proximity, it is the baby's alternative to fur-clinging.

Many mothers believe that the baby learns to smile by imitating their own grinning faces but this is not so. Smiling is an inborn reaction and babies would start smiling regardless of anything their mothers did or did not do. We know this for certain because even babies born blind, who can never see their mothers' faces, start smiling automatically when they reach the age of four weeks. Smiling is too important a human signal for anything to be left to chance.

Smiling is not the only facial expression to have its roots in infancy. The baby's most vital activity in its earliest months is sucking at the breast. This involves pushing the lips forward in a gentle pout. There is no tension here, as there is when angry lips move forward. The lips are soft and the teeth, when formed, are covered. This expression survives into adult life as the loving kiss.

Unlike the smile, the softly protruded lips are not uniquely human. This is something we share with other primates. Watch any young chimpanzee seeking gentle contact and you will see its long, muscular lips pull forward into a super-pout. And when chimpanzees greet one another they often press their lips onto the companion's hand or body in a way that is amazingly human. If you ever encounter a chimpanzee, the correct way to greet it is to stretch out a limp hand and offer the back of it to be kissed. If friendly, the ape will press its mouth softly against your knuckles. This is remarkably reminiscent of the hand kiss that was employed in polite human society for many centuries and which is still visible today in certain cultures, especially if that other distinguished primate, the Pope, happens to be involved.

When the infant is put to the breast it must do more than just suck. It must first home in on the nipple. Most mothers place their infant's lips right next to the nipple but in making the final adjustment with its lips, the baby can often be seen to move its head up and down in a searching movement. This up and down action means '*Yes*, I am hungry and I want to feed'. Again, it is a movement that survives into adult life as an important gesture: the head nod. This is why most people around the world nod their heads up and down when they want to say YES.

When the baby has finished feeding, it rejects the breast in one of two ways: it either twists its head to one side or it raises it up. Both actions remove its mouth from the region of the nipple. As before, these actions have survived as adult gestures. The twisting of the head to the side becomes the sideways head shake meaning NO. Most people in the world perform this lateral head shake when saying NO but in one area they do not. In the Greek region, they use another gesture for NO. They base it not on the infant's sideways twist of the head but on its upwards tilt. The Greek NO is an upward head toss.

Some observers were surprised to find that the Greek head toss was also being used in southern Italy. People living in Rome and to the north used the ordinary head shake, like the rest of Europe, but Neapolitans and those in the south employed the Greek head toss. Why should this be? The answer lies in ancient history: about two and a half thousand years ago the Greeks colonized southern Italy and left their mark upon its culture. Even their gestures survived, untouched by the long passage of time. What is more, they left a 'gesture frontier' – a line between Rome and Naples where their head toss gives way to the northern head shake. This line is in the region of the Massico mountain range and it is an amazing fact that this is precisely where the Greeks halted their expansion in the region, over two thousand years ago. Today, the gestures of Italian people still respect that ancient frontier, despite the mobility of modern populations. Body language, clearly, can be highly conservative.

Some gestures are so ancient that it is hard to trace their origins. In Britain the worst gestural insult you can make is to raise your hand, with the palm towards your face and with the first and second fingers held up in a V-shape. Everyone knows this gesture but few can agree as to why it should be so insulting. Its origins have been forgotten. Outside Britain it is hardly known and is confused with the cheerful V for victory sign. To the British there is a clear distinction between the two: the victory sign is always made with the palm of the hand facing forward, easily distinguishing it from the palm-back insult V. In other countries no such distinction is made. There, a V-sign means victory regardless of the direction of the palm.

When Britons were asked to explain why their insult V should be so rude, they gave no fewer than ten different explanations of the symbolism involved, including such imaginative interpretations as 'a double penis', 'spread female legs', 'open female genitals' and 'a female pubic triangle'. They were all guessing. According to historians who have investigated this gesture, it can be traced back to a single incident in the year 1415 when, before the battle of Agincourt, the French made a savage threat against the English archers, who had been causing them so much trouble. When they won the battle, the French announced, they would celebrate by cutting off the 'bow fingers' (the first and second fingers that were used to draw back the bow) of all the defeated English archers, preventing them from ever firing another arrow. Henry V was astute enough to warn his archers of this threat, just before the battle began, thereby considerably increasing their enthusiasm for the fight. Later that day, after the English had gained a memorable victory, the captive Frenchmen were ridiculed by the English archers, who taunted them by holding aloft their – still attached – bow fingers.

This, it is claimed, is the origin of the famous insult V-sign and it is surprising that it has survived for centuries when almost everyone has forgotten its true meaning. Part of the reason is that the upward jerking of the fingers has an essentially phallic quality that lends itself to an insulting role. Because of this, people using it today think that it is in some way sexual, which helps to keep it alive as an obscenity.

There is a related insult gesture, known from ancient Roman times, that has a genuinely

Many local gestures have an ancient origin. The V for victory sign, with the palm facing forward, is well known all over the world, but in Britain if the V-sign is made the other way around, with the palm back, it is a gross insult. This version can be traced back to the 15th century when the French threatened to cut off the bow fingers of the English archers. After the English had won the battle they insulted the French by holding their two bow fingers aloft.

The phallic middle-finger gesture is one of the most ancient insults known. It was popular in early Rome, and the emperor Caligula, when allowing his subjects to kiss his hand, is said to have offered them his middle finger as a deliberate way of creating a scandal.

Some rude gestures, such as thumbing the nose, are widely understood, but others are local. In Greece, the 'Moutza' gesture, with the open palm pushed towards the victim, is such an extreme insult that it is even used as a car sticker to enrage the driver following you. It stems from an ancient Byzantine custom of pushing filth into the faces of tethered criminals, but to non-Greeks it simply looks like a mild 'go back' sign.

phallic origin – the middle-finger jerk – in which only this digit is erected and thrust upward into the air. It was so famous in ancient times that this central finger was then known as the 'obscene digit' or 'infamous digit'. This gesture has survived for two thousand years and its existence may well have influenced the phallic interpretation of the British insult V-sign.

In Greece a completely different, ancient sign takes over as the major insult gesture. This is the 'Moutza', a Byzantine hand movement in which the palm, with fingers spread, is thrust towards the face of the victim. To the rest of the world this looks like a simple 'go back' gesture but to the Greeks it is a serious affront. Its origin can be traced to the days when captives were put on display in the streets and a passer-by would pick up a handful of filth and thrust it in the hapless prisoner's face. So the Moutza gesture says 'I throw filth in your face', although to most modern Greeks this origin is long forgotten. They, too, now see it as an obscene gesture and have given it their own, modern explanation. Not knowing how it began, they have invented a sexual interpretation, seeing the five displayed digits as symbolic of the five worst sexual practices that could be inflicted upon the female relatives of their victim.

It seems that, once a gesture has become entrenched in a culture, it becomes unusually tenacious. If it needs a little extra support to keep it going, people will invent reasons for using it. By reading new meanings into it they will give it fresh life. Today, for example, the ancient, Byzantine Moutza gesture can be purchased in Greece as a plastic car sticker, to provide a permanent insult to all drivers following too closely behind.

Even more ancient than the Moutza gesture is the fig sign. In this, the hand is closed and the thumb is squeezed between the first two fingers, with only its tip showing. It was meant to represent the female genitals and was employed as a protective gesture. It may seem strange to us today to employ an explicitly sexual sign as a defence against ill fortune but this superstitious strategy was once commonplace.

The practice can be traced back to ancient Greece, where women would, under certain special circumstances, ritually expose their genitals as a way of breaking magic spells. This curious action was even depicted in later times on stone carvings above the doors of certain Christian churches. It was based on the idea that evil spirits could be distracted by showing them sexual organs and, once their attention had been diverted, their spell (whatever it happened to be) would be broken. The fig gesture (in Italian, the '*mano fica*' – *fica* or fig being a slang term for the female genitals) is a symbolic version of this ancient, religious act of exhibitionism. By Roman times it was a popular custom to wear a little amulet showing a hand making the fig sign. The wearer was then permanently protected from evil spirits.

Today most people use the gesture as a rude sexual comment or insult and have forgotten its original, protective role. But strangely, in one European country, its original function has survived. In Portugal the fig gesture remains to this day as a protective sign without any hint of obscenity. This also applies to Brazil, with its strong Portuguese influences, and to certain other places touched by Portugal during the height of its colonial powers.

Once, when, in the interests of scientific research, I was visiting a geisha house in Kyoto, I was amazed to find that the geisha girls there used the fig sign as a protection. It seemed inconceivable that such a specific gesture could have arisen independently and I was baffled by its appearance in Japan, thousands of miles away from its European source, until I was gently reminded that it had been the Portuguese who were the first Europeans to visit Japan, back in the 1540s. It seems that they must have traded gestures as well as goods on those pioneering visits. This is not so surprising when one considers the enormous linguistic problems early travellers must have faced during their hazardous voyages to unknown lands. Body language must have been of even greater importance on such occasions. With the fig sign it appeared that, once again, an early gesture had survived for centuries without altering its form or its meaning. Sometimes, however, a slight change does take place as time passes and this modification can obscure the origin of a particular gesture.

*In earlier days, some sexual gestures were used, not as obscenities, but as protections against evil spirits. The idea was that a sexual sign would divert the attention of the evil forces. It may come as a shock to the more pious churchgoers of the British Isles to discover that on the outside walls of some of their Christian churches there are images of women holding open their genitals. This example comes from Kilpeck in Herefordshire.*

In modern Hawaii, for instance, there is a special local greeting in which the right hand is held aloft with the thumb and the little finger erect. The other three fingers are bent forward. With the hand in this position, the Hawaiian wags it gently in the air. It is the gestural equivalent of 'Aloha!'.

Visiting the islands, I asked the local inhabitants where this gesture had come from but nobody could tell me. It was 'just traditional' – the usual reply when origins have been forgotten. Spurred on by the fact that nobody else in the world uses this particular form of greeting, I set out to trace its roots.

The answer was unexpected. It turned out to be a modified Spanish gesture. At some point in the history of the Hawaiian islands, Spanish sailors, or immigrants from the Spanish cultures of Central or South America, must have brought it with them. On arrival they no doubt wished to show they were friendly by inviting the locals to join them for a drink. In early days Spaniards drank out of small leather bottles which they held up to their mouths so that a jet of liquid was poured straight into their open lips. Tourists in Spain today are sometimes encouraged to drink the local wine in this ancient manner, possibly because the novelty of the action makes them forget the quality of the drink they are being offered. And even today, the Spanish (and South American) gesture for 'come and have a drink' is a mime of the action of tilting up a leather bottle.

The gesture consists of erecting the thumb and little finger and then pointing the thumb towards the open lips. This must have been the action that those early Spanish-speaking visitors made towards the local Hawaiians when they arrived upon their shores. The Hawaiians learned its friendly meaning and began to imitate it. But because it now stood for 'friendly greeting' rather than 'come and have a drink', they omitted the directional element of the gesture. Instead of pointing the thumb towards the lips, they simply held the hand aloft and waggled it back and forth, combining the Spanish drinking gesture with a cheerful wave. As time passed, the old form of the gesture was gradually forgotten, until it became known simply as the local greeting. And today nobody realizes that when they make this gesture they are using a Spanish drinking signal hundreds of years old. Again, this proves how conservative body language can be.

It also demonstrates a major communication problem that can arise with certain gestures. They can develop a local meaning that is not understood elsewhere. Unconscious actions,

In Hawaii there is a local greeting sign with the thumb and little finger held out. In origin this is an ancient Spanish drinking gesture. When aimed at the lips it mimics the action of drinking from a leather bottle, but in Hawaii today it has lost any connection with the mouth.

Some gestures have many meanings. In America (above) the ring sign means OK; in southern France it signifies zero or worthless; in the Middle East it is an obscenity and in Japan (below) it stands for money. For travellers and tourists it is easy to make mistakes.

like the gesticulations we make when speaking, or our common facial expressions, are understood worldwide. But when specific, deliberate gestures are invented, to replace speech, they can easily develop special regional meanings which may cause considerable confusion. One gesture can mean completely different things in different countries.

A few examples will show just how dangerous this can be. If an Italian touches his ear-lobe, he is saying to a man 'you are a pansy . . . you should be wearing earrings'. In a fiercely heterosexual context, to suggest that a man is effeminate can easily lead to explosive violence and has even resulted in killings. Pity the poor Portuguese tourist who wanders into a bar and makes this gesture. For him, back home, touching the ear-lobe is a signal that something is especially good, excellent, magnificent! He buys a drink in an Italian bar and is asked by the barman if he likes it. He replies with his 'excellent' ear touch but to the man behind the bar he is saying 'clear off, you simpering pansy'. The outcome is predictable.

If the Portuguese tourist retreated nearer to home, he would still not be out of trouble for, even as close as neighbouring Spain, the ear touch has a completely different significance. To the Spaniard it indicates that someone is a 'sponger' and never pays for his drinks. He leaves his companions 'hanging there like an ear-lobe'. In other countries this gesture can act as a threat, meaning 'I will box your ears' or 'I will pull you by the ear'.

The familiar American OK sign, with the thumb and forefinger making a ring, is understood as a 'good' sign by many people. But not by all. In certain regions – Sardinia, for instance, or the Middle East – to make this sign is a foul obscenity, with the ring shape standing for one of the more private orifices of the human body. If you are asked what you thought of the meal and you make this gesture, you may not be saying 'great!' but 'up yours', a response that is bound to puzzle any sensitive chef.

Even in France the gesture is not always safe, for in the south it can mean 'zero' or 'worthless'. Here the symbolism of the ring is based on the nought and suggests that something is a big zero. If you are asked about the wine and you reply 'excellent' with the ring sign, you are in fact saying the vintage is worthless.

In Japan the confusion continues because there the ring sign means money and you may be thought to be requesting a small loan when all you wish to do is to say that all is well.

Hitch-hikers can also be at risk in foreign countries. In parts of the Mediterranean region the friendly, jerked thumb that is normally used when begging for a lift can cause considerable offence. If a driver stops in response to this signal it may not be to offer a ride but to punch the hitch-hiker on the nose. This is because, in those regions, the jerked thumb signal means 'sit on this'.

There are many such examples of serious confusion where symbolic gestures are involved. The reason is simple. Because we all understand the less deliberate, more spontaneous gesticulations and facial expressions, we assume that all forms of body language are the same the world over. We know perfectly well that foreign spoken languages will be different from our own, and we make allowances for that, but we naively imagine that visual body languages will not.

In reality there are two distinct kinds of gesture: those which we are hardly aware of and we all share, and those which we use deliberately in place of speech and which have a special, local history. The former act like animal signals, the latter like foreign words.

This does not only apply to foreign gestures. Even the seemingly simplest action may have different local meanings. What could be simpler than the gesture of the beckoning hand, meaning 'come here'? Surely everyone will understand that? Not so. In fact a misunderstanding about a 'simple' beckon once caused two deaths.

The problem arose because northern Europeans beckon in a different way from southern Europeans. In the north the hand is held palm up when it beckons. In the south the action is performed palm down. To the Northerner the southern beckon looks like a 'go back', 'go away' sign, and this is what led to a tragic accident.

One sunny afternoon two strong swimmers had left their crowded, Mediterranean holiday beach and had set off on a long swim to a nearby shore, little knowing that it was the site of a secret military establishment. Armed guards patrolling the shoreline saw them coming and, fearing that they might be spies, beckoned to them to come ashore for interrogation. The swimmers, who came from northern Europe, noticed the palm-down arm movements, saw the guns the guards were carrying and immediately realized that they had strayed into a restricted zone. They were also convinced that the guards were signalling to them to 'go back, go back', so they quickly turned and started to swim away. The guards assumed from this that they were indeed spies and were trying to escape, and shot them dead. Gestures may be simple but they are far from trivial.

A more subtle misunderstanding takes place over and over again when business people from different cultures meet at conferences. They are there for friendly discussion but cannot understand why they feel so ill at ease with their foreign colleagues. A little quiet observation soon reveals why this is. We each come from a culture that has an unwritten 'standing rule'. This rule states that when we are engaged in normal conversation we should stand at a particular distance from our companions. We learn this slowly as we grow up and we acquire a 'comfortable standing distance' without ever realizing it. It is automatic for us to settle into this distance and, by the time we are sophisticated adults, we do so effortlessly and unconsciously. The catch is that our colleagues, who have done the same thing, may come from a culture that has arrived at a different comfort-distance from our own.

Take, for example, an important diplomatic meeting between British and Arab officials who have gathered to discuss the price of oil, or peace in the Middle East. The British come from a 'fingertips' culture – that is to say, one that feels comfortable when standing at about arm's reach from their companions. The Arabs come from an 'elbow' culture – one that only feels comfortable when standing twice as close, at about half-arm's length.

As the discussions begin in earnest, the Arabs advance until they are only half an arm away from the British officials. Now the Arabs feel comfortable. But the British feel threatened: the Arabs seem to be bearing down on them aggressively. So they move back until they are at full-arm distance. Now the British feel at ease but the Arabs feel rejected. So they move in close again until they are, once more, feeling comfortable. Again, the British feel threatened and withdraw a little further. And all around the room, at diplomatic meetings of this kind, one can observe retreating British officials pinned to the walls by advancing Arabs, both sides feeling ill at ease without knowing quite why and with the friendly discussions needlessly disrupted.

There is more to social gatherings than mere body distance, however. Even when we are among friends from our own culture and feel at ease spatially, there are other under-currents of body language operating. If our social relationships are well balanced, this will be reflected in the similarity of our unspoken body postures and movements. If our relations are poor, our body signals will differ.

Careful observations of close friends talking together have revealed that they frequently adopt what is called 'postural echo' and 'movement synchrony'. Without being aware of what they are doing, they adjust themselves so that, if one shifts into a particular position, the companion follows suit. In this way the posture of one tends to 'echo' the posture of the other. What is more, the shifts occur at almost exactly the same time, creating a rough kind of body synchrony. If, on the other hand, the relations between the two are strained, the echo and the synchrony are absent. Then the pair feel strangely edgy in one another's company.

We often smile at the stylized movements of synchronized swimmers, formation dancers or goose-stepping soldiers. The rigid way in which the members of these groups copy one another's every move seems highly unnatural to us. But the truth is that we are all subtly synchronized, every day of our social lives, without realizing it. At a party we can be observed drinking together, shifting our bodies together, smiling together and tossing back our heads and laughing together. We may think that we are each responding individually to a particular action but this is not the case. We tune our reactions to minute clues from our companions' bodies, which tell us precisely when to shift our legs or throw back our heads. This synchrony is important because it plays a secret role in making us feel good. It makes us part of the tribe, one of the gang, and gives special value to our social mixing.

The loner, the one out of step with these body 'matchings', will miss the sense of belonging and will be forced into a special social role – that of rebel, misfit or outsider. Loners may be able to comment on the group and its behaviour but they will never be part of it.

In situations where the sense of belonging is especially important, the members of a group may find themselves performing actions so precisely synchronized that they appear almost as rigid in their group adherence as the marching soldiers or the formation dancers. And yet they achieve this without any training or formal agreement. This can be seen at a pop concert, where all the hands wave in the air together, or at a football match, where the so-called 'disorganized rabble' clap their hands in complex rhythms that are synchronized to within one-sixteenth of a second of one another. For the young, shared group experiences of this kind have deep significance in moulding their social attitudes. For this reason, they sometimes alarm the authorities, who would prefer all group bondings to be subservient to their political control.

When people are
like-minded, they are
often like-bodied. They
demonstrate their shared
feelings by synchronizing
their behaviour. This is
frequently seen when a
huge crowd gathers at a
sporting event or a pop
concert.

Body language is much more influential than most people recognize. It infiltrates every human interaction and provides a revealing, subliminal commentary on what is officially taking place. The main reason it is so important is because it is more truthful than the official elements of our social encounters. We lie much more easily with our spoken words than with our expressions, our gesticulations and our body postures. True, we can put on a good face, we can muster up a false smile and we can pretend to be annoyed. We can be deceitful with our actions as well as with our words but only when we know what we are doing. We know what words we are speaking, so that we can control our utterances down to the last syllable, but what are our fingers doing as we speak? How are our feet shifting as we talk? We may be able to control and manipulate some of our gestures but not all of them. There are too many and we are too preoccupied with what we are saying to be able to concentrate on all the finer points of our bodily actions.

Some individuals – such as great actors and devious politicians – do become extremely adept at lying with their bodies. They often fool us, and we believe them. They manage to avoid what has been called 'non-verbal leakage' – something that most of us do every day. Despite our attempts to suppress tell-tale signs, we give the game away by leaking little bits of information as we speak. We do this in several ways.

When we are telling lies we gesticulate less. This is because, unconsciously, we sense that if we use our hands their actions may not fit with our words. Our hands may be clenching tight, for example, when we are cooing soft words of love. Or they may flutter limply while our words insist that we are taking a firm stand. So we intuitively reduce our hand movements. But this in itself then becomes a clue that deception is taking place. It may not be easy to spot but to a trained eye it is clear enough.

Although the liar is less likely to wave his hands about in the air, he is more likely to use them in other ways. When deception is taking place he feels a strange compulsion to touch his face. Every so often one or both hands move up towards his mouth, as if trying to mask the lie that is issuing from his lips. Once there, another fleeting sensation takes over – the feeling that covering the mouth is too obvious. So the hand moves on and rubs the cheek, strokes the nose, scratches the eyebrow or touches the forehead. This attempt to cover up the cover-up usually works well. The companion imagines that the speaker's nose must be itching and ignores the trivial action, while continuing to listen to the honeyed words. But if he were to compare truthful conversations with untruthful ones, he would be astonished at how much more frequently his companion's face 'felt itchy' when deception was taking place.

I am sometimes challenged on this point by people who say, 'But supposing the nose really is itching?' The answer is to study the scratching. Someone who has been stung by an insect or who has a runny nose or an irritating pimple on his cheek, will scratch in a more intense, specific way than the liar. The liar's hand-to-face actions are almost casual by comparison. They are token scratches, half-hearted rubs, small actions which lack conviction. Again, to the trained eye, the difference is not hard to spot.

There is one particular hand posture that increases when deception is taking place: the hand shrug. The hands are held in front of the body, palm up and with the fingers slightly curled. The degree of curling increases little by little from the first finger to the fourth. Some observers have been puzzled as to why this particular action should increase when someone is lying. The answer is to be found in the message that is transmitted during ordinary shrugging. The full shrug, with shoulders raised, mouth corners pulled down, head tilted, eyes turned up and hands held out, is used as a disclaimer: 'I don't know', 'I can't help', 'I don't understand'. It is always a negative message, in which the gesturer essentially is saying, 'This has nothing to do with me'. When people start to lie, they unconsciously want to distance themselves from what they are doing and their small hand shrug is the tell-tale clue.

Another form of non-verbal leakage is the body shift. When we are telling the truth we may wave our hands about, we may even lean forward, or leap up, but we do not squirm. The bad liar does squirm a little, his body showing a strong urge to escape, while held firmly in place by the need to brazen out the lie. The good liar manages to suppress most of this body shifting but not all. There are nearly always a few tiny body movements left that he finds it impossible to eliminate. They may be no more than a slight shift of weight or pressure but they can be spotted if the listener is alert to them.

All these tell-tale signs can be observed not only in people who are in the process of telling lies but also when they are momentarily silent. Then, the gestures must be interpreted in a slightly different way. If, for example, somebody is asked a difficult question – one that he does not wish to answer – he may touch his nose or shift the weight of his body before he replies. What is happening is that, while he is thinking about the question and how to answer it, he appears calm but his brain is seething. That is the deception: outward calm, inward panic. When he finally does reply he may be lying or he may in fact be telling the truth.

So caution must be used when interpreting these small 'leaks' in our body language. They certainly indicate that something is going on inside the brain of the companion that is not being shown to the outside world but whether this amounts to a downright lie or a moment of soul-searching followed by a difficult truth will vary from case to case. Despite this weakness, however, non-verbal leakage does provide valuable clues about how simple and straightforward a companion is being in any particular encounter, or how complex and devious he is.

Clearly, the visual language of the body is a powerful communication system that is slightly less under our control than we imagine. The reason is not hard to find. So many elements are performed unconsciously that they inevitably reveal our innermost feelings. No matter how self-conscious we become, for much of the time we remain unaware of what our faces, hands and feet are doing as we engage in conversation. At best, we can only recall in the vaguest terms how we were gesticulating or grimacing as we spoke.

There are so many occasions when we wish to hide our true feelings that our body language is often more of an embarrassment than an advantage. The doctor who must conceal unpleasant facts from an anxious patient, the salesman who must mask his hostility towards an irritating customer, the hostess who must appear pleased to see unwanted guests, the job candidate who must hide his nervousness from his interviewer – all of these people must do their best to eliminate tell-tale body signs that give the game away.

Nowhere is the suppression of body language more important, however, than in the sphere of professional poker. In this essentially simple card game, large sums of money are won and lost according to the bluffing ability of the individual players. A player who can conceal his pleasure at a good hand or his disappointment at a bad one is able to turn his self-control into considerable profit.

To observe this form of self-discipline at its very best, a visit to Binion's Horseshoe Casino in Las Vegas is needed. There, once a year, the World Series of Poker is held, a contest that attracts masters of the game from all over the world. It is a knockout

From time to time we all attempt to suppress our body language in order to hide our feelings. For international poker players this becomes a way of life. At the World Poker Contest in Las Vegas, the best exponents of the 'poker face' can be observed at close quarters. Two hundred and twenty competitors begin the contest but at the end of four days' play there are only two left with one million dollars in cash stacked on the table to be won or lost on the final hand.

competition starting with 220 players. Each puts in a stake of ten thousand dollars and play begins. After three days there are only six players left in and the tension becomes almost unbearable. On the fourth day these six must sit around a single table and play until only two remain. At this point armed guards bring in a million dollars in cash and pile it up in the middle of the table. Play continues, watched by television cameras and a huge crowd, until, finally, one of the two has lost all his chips and the survivor, on that final deal of cards, wins the whole mountain of a million dollars. Never has the pressure to conceal human emotions been greater.

So how do the top players manage it? They appear to use three different techniques. First, and most common, is the Statue Strategy. This involves complete immobility. The face is deadpan throughout and the eyes are often concealed by dark glasses and a peaked cap. The body is stiff and rigid. The hands make the absolute minimum of movement, just enough to inspect the cards and to place the bets. Both these actions are done with studied efficiency. The way the chips are placed in the centre of the table never varies. The way the hands touch and turn the cards up for secret inspection is always performed with identical, functional actions. There are no flourishes, no grimaces, nothing. It is like playing with a machine, a carefully programmed robot.

The second strategy is what might be called the False Clown. This is rare and is disliked by the other players. The exact opposite of the Statue Strategy, it involves a non-stop display of acting. The idea is to provide so much body language that it is impossible for the opponents to detect the true mood beneath the surface bluster. Some individuals are mock-aggressive, others mock-friendly. Some are jokey, others sexually suggestive. They deliberately rile the other players and hope to make them lose their cool.

The third strategy is the most demanding of all. This consists of Erratic Signalling. The player openly shows delight and dismay at the cards he receives but manages to ensure that his display of emotions bears no relationship to the true quality of his cards. This is a dangerous device and requires great acting ability but if done well can be wonderfully confusing for the other players.

Because all of these three techniques can be highly efficient at hiding the truth, the top players know that they must find special ways of seeing through them. They must watch out for small, tell-tale signs that even good players cannot suppress completely. These signs are known as 'tells' and have been studied extensively by poker experts. The most useful tells are as follows:

1  When looking at his cards, a player will stare longer at a bad hand than at a good one.

2  If his hand excites him, his blink rate will increase as he stares at his cards. Eye-shades and dark glasses obscure this 'tell'.

3  If he has good cards, he will be unable to prevent pupil dilation, the small black spot at the centre of each eye growing visibly in size. Again, dark glasses can mask this automatic reaction.

4  If he has a good hand, he is likely to look away after staring at his cards and will not engage in eye contact with other players. If he stares assertively at other players he probably has a bad hand.

5  If he has a good hand, he will glance for a split second at his pile of chips before looking away.

6  If he has a bad hand, he will make his bet with an exaggerated flourish. If he has a good hand, he will move his chips forward in a quiet, precise way.

These are some of the most common 'tells'. In general, the player with a good hand attempts to reduce his involvement – staring only briefly at the cards, looking away from the other players and making his bet neatly with an inconspicuous arm movement.

Top players are able to conceal or control even these tiny give-away signs. Ordinary players are unable to control these small details of their body language and will eventually lose their money. In the 1993 contest, the winner – from Arizona – was so completely deadpan throughout the competition that he found it difficult to return to ordinary body language. After four gruelling days of intense play, when he had finally won the million dollars, his face refused to show any emotion. Immediately after his moment of triumph he stood up and walked to the centre of the room. There, still deadpan, he stabbed his right forefinger into the air in a symbolic *coup de grâce*. As he turned away, his face remained expressionless. Only when he moved across to the side of the arena and was embraced by his excited wife and daughter did he, at long last, allow himself a broad, triumphant smile.

In some cultures the suppression of body language takes a special form. It becomes a display of social class. Instead of the suppression being switched on when needed, to conceal inner emotions, it is a permanent state of public conduct. We have all heard of the British stiff upper lip, the inscrutability of the Oriental and the stone-face cool of the macho cowboy. For such people the act of self-control becomes a sign of high status. The dominant male, in particular, does not allow himself to show his feelings.

This kind of cultural suppression has a long history. For century after century there have been strong verbal attacks on those who gesture too freely. In the seventeenth century, for instance, the French were mocked for their 'many shrugs and Apish gestures' and the Italians for the 'unseemly and ridiculous' way that they were seen to 'wag their hands up and down very often'. In some countries specific instructions were given to men of standing, requiring them to control their movements in public places. According to some authorities, becoming civilized and exerting self-control were one and the same. Only the brutish lower classes were permitted to gesture freely when expressing their emotions.

For some reason, this body-control ruling applied much more strongly in northern Europe than in the south and this difference has survived even to the present day. Southern Italians gesticulate far more than northern Italians and southern Frenchmen do so more than Parisians in the north. All around the Mediterranean the gestures fly thick and fast. In northern Europe the more stoical figure remains the norm, although this is less obvious among the young.

There is an underlying, biological reason for high status being associated with body control. A dominant ape, monkey or wolf shows less body movement than its subordinates. The top animal in any group has an almost calm stillness in its demeanour and need do no more than cast a withering glance at an unruly subordinate to make an impact. The top male can afford this stillness because he has already proved himself. He does not need to burn up energy with body language. His mere presence is enough.

It is this 'coolness' of the dominant animal that is at the basis of social body control in human societies. Calm self-discipline carries with it an automatic quality of power and dominance. It spells confidence and the lack of any need to pander to companions or curry their favour.

Today, in our increasingly egalitarian societies, it is rare to find anyone, even among the richest and most powerful figures, who is able to conduct himself or herself with total body restraint and aloofness. They must always consider the possibility that, despite their privileged position, they could be ousted if sufficient public pressure was brought to bear. For this reason modern-day monarchs and heads of state can often be seen to perform a number of tell-tale signs of apprehension or mild anxiety when attending major events.

A classical anxiety signal is given by many top figures at the moment when they arrive at a formal gathering and must walk across an open space to be greeted by their hosts. As they do so, they perform what is called a 'barrier signal'. They create a protective 'buffer' across the front of the body. Males usually do this by tugging at a cuff or adjusting a cufflink or wrist-watch. Needless to say, the cuff, cufflink and watch are all in perfect order and require no last-minute improvements but by the act of touching them the dominant figure is able to construct a 'body-cross' – an arm barrier across the front of the body. Just as the bumper or fender of a car protects it from minor collisions, so the body-cross gives the celebrity a sense that he is protected from those around him. It is a small comfort action which, disguised as clothing adjustment, usually goes unnoticed and unremarked.

Top females arriving at such events, and lacking cufflinks, frequently adjust the position of a handbag on a forearm, or make some other minor costume shift that magically brings an arm up as an unconscious defence against the tensions of the moment.

To find a dominant figure free of all such actions today, it is necessary to search far and wide. Where on earth would such a person be ruling the roost in motionless, expressionless, aloof calm? The answer is at the headquarters of giant corporations. There, at the very top of the pyramid of power, it is still possible to find individuals with an almost medieval power. These are people who have no fears where their subordinates are concerned, who rule with complete autocratic power and need therefore show no apprehension or sociable bodily communication. In Japan, especially, the top men of the vast industrial companies can be seen sitting as still as statues and walking as if in a private dream. The rest of us sit down; they sit. The rest of us interact; they receive. The rest of us are alert and responsive; they are stiffly serene.

Such people remind us of the true value of our day-by-day body language. Nearly all our body signals have to do with smoothing the path of daily life, making it a little easier to deal with the rough and tumble of social encounters. The shared smile, the friendly wave, the nod of approval, the attentive gaze and all the rest of our huge repertoire of

When we feel slightly apprehensive we unconsciously protect ourselves by forming a barrier across the front of our body. This 'body-cross' action, in which one arm comes across to make contact with the other, is performed even by the most dominant social figures when they must negotiate an open space on a formal occasion.

small, fleeting, visual signals add up to a vitally important system of social cooperation. For most human beings, daily existence is full of minor fears and worries, uncertainties and stresses, and we need all the help we can get. The body language of our companions reassures us by showing us that we are not alone with these problems – that we all experience the same dilemmas and doubts.

Our daily existence is also full of small pleasures and rewards, and these can be greatly enhanced by sharing them with others. The value of social feedback is so great that the worst punishment we can give to a prisoner is to place him in solitary confinement.

Our verbal language has, as its primary function, the exchange of factual information. Its secondary role is to act as a channel for expressing our emotions. With our body language the situation is reversed. Its primary function is to reveal our moods.

We have designed computers to improve the efficiency of our information exchange. Computers carry a mass of verbal language but they have no body language. Computers never smile, even when you type a good joke onto their screens. By contrast, our body language has been given no new technological boost. It has remained untouched by the advance of civilization. It survives as a wonderful, primeval relic in the midst of our modern cities, ensuring that in a cold machine age we remain warmly human.

To watch it is to witness a fascinating human ballet of gestures and expressions, of postures and movements, an everyday ballet in which the performers need no training. And since so much of it is shared by all humanity, it remains one of the most important aids to unifying our species that have have left today.

It is true that there are many local gestures that cause confusion but there are many more that do not. Put two people without a common spoken language in the same room and they will soon be communicating with one another by means of body language. A smile, a pointed finger, a mimed action of drinking, and already a small bond has been forged. With only their separate verbal languages to help them, they would be unable to bridge the divide between them. But with their shared body language they can start to build a simple human relationship.

It is this that makes the language of the body so crucial to our future on this planet. For years people have looked upon gestures as a trivial, minor subject. Linguistics, the study of the spoken and written word, has, on the other hand, been feted as a major topic. Yet it is spoken language that divides the world and body language that unites it. Our spoken languages, so vital at serving communication within each culture, have developed such huge differences over time that they have become a major source of cultural separation. They have helped to convert each nation into something approaching a separate 'species'.

By definition, different species are groups of animals that do not interbreed. Because of the great differences in spoken languages, the chances of people marrying across the language barrier are greatly reduced. It does happen, of course, but usually only when one partner has learned the language of the other and therefore destroyed the barrier. But the number of couples that live and breed together without speaking a word of one another's verbal language is extremely small. Their common body language might enable them to share a few loving days but soon the need for detailed information exchange would become increasingly frustrated. The splitting off of the different tongues has resulted in verbal language becoming one of the major *anti*-communication systems of our species.

There are great dangers in such divisions, as we all know, and this makes the unifying potential of our globally shared body language even more significant for the future of our species. Brave attempts to introduce a universal tongue – Esperanto – have failed dismally but those who saw that movement as the only hope for peaceful coexistence need not be too depressed. As long as we can smile at one another, laugh, embrace, hug, point and nod, there is hope for a friendly future.

The more I travel the globe making observations of the language of the human body, the more optimistic I become. Everyone talks about the irreconcilable differences that exist between nations and cultures and societies but, by contrast, I see so many similarities, so many shared emotions and common moods. When two old men meet and pat one another on the back, when a triumphant sportsman flings his arms high in the air or when two girls giggle shyly together, casting sidelong glances at a boy, the expressions and actions I observe could belong to any culture on earth and be understood by them all, without a word being spoken.

If this is the case, then why do we witness so much antagonism, so much violence and so many angry disputes? If we share so much, what is it that keeps us at one another's throats? To understand that, it is necessary to re-examine the way in which our species evolved and to ask the fundamental question: what kind of creature is the human animal?

# 2

# *The Hunting Ape*

'There are one hundred and ninety-three living species of monkeys and apes. One hundred and ninety-two of them are covered with hair. The exception is a naked ape self-named *Homo sapiens*. This unusual and highly successful species spends a great deal of time examining his higher motives and an equal amount of time studiously ignoring his fundamental ones. He is proud that he has the biggest brain of all the primates but attempts to conceal the fact that he also has the biggest penis ... He is an intensely vocal, acutely exploratory, over-crowded ape and it is high time we examined his basic behaviour.'

That is how I introduced a book that I wrote back in the 1960s, for which I received a great deal of criticism. It was based on a simple premise: I am a zoologist and human beings are animals – so why should I not write about them in the same way that I had done with other animals?

This seemed logical enough to me but it outraged many people. They felt that human beings do not belong to nature, that we are somehow special and above natural laws, protected by some unseen super-being. I felt that we are very much a part of nature and not above it; that we are just another animal species – an extraordinary one, true, but an animal all the same. Above all, I was sure that we are protected only by our own abilities. They believed in an after-life, I believed in life.

To drive home my point I called the book *The Naked Ape* and in it I referred to human beings only by that name. I needed to shock people into seeing themselves as they really are, rather than as they pretend to be.

I was attacked by the Church for ignoring the human soul. I argued that the only true hope of immortality for human beings was to be found in their reproductive organs, where the potentially eternal genetical material lies embedded. I was attacked by the puritans for describing human sexuality honestly and pointing out, with scientific accuracy, that we are the sexiest primate alive. And, rather amusingly, I was attacked by the psychologists, anthropologists and sociologists, who took offence at my zoological intrusion into what they considered their private territory.

I was not used to this sort of attention. When I wrote about fish or birds or snakes, nobody was upset. But when I wrote in the same way about people, the roof fell in. Clearly mankind's enlarged brain has given the species a badly swollen head.

The comments I heard confirmed this. I was said to be degrading humankind, to be making man beastly. This surprised me because I like animals and I feel proud to call myself one. I have never looked down upon them and so for me to call human beings naked apes is not degrading, it is simply being honest and putting us in our place as part of the scheme of nature on this planet.

What had nudged me closer to my zoological view of mankind were my studies, in the 1950s, of our closest living relatives, the African chimpanzees. I was astonished at how advanced they were, at how subtle and complex their behaviour was, and I could see how easy it must have been to pass over the threshold from chimpdom to humanity ... a small step for a chimp, a giant leap for mankind.

How we took that leap is still a hotly debated topic. Why? Because, as the first law of scientific discussion states: 'The less light that has been thrown on a subject the more heat it generates.' The simple, plain truth is that we have no hard evidence at all as to how our remote ancestors came to shed their hairy coats, stand on their hind legs and talk their heads off. There is a gap of several million years in the fossil record, when we can only guess at what took place.

This dark age of humanity is known as the Pliocene Gap and occurred between about four and seven million years ago. Apes went into it and ape-men came out of it. How these ape-men then went on to become modern men is no mystery. There is no 'missing link' in the popular sense. We have a whole series of fossils tracing our ancestry back to the primeval ape-men but beyond them, in the crucial formative stage, the picture becomes vague.

The traditional view – and it is only a guess – is that our ancestors left the cover of the forests for the open plains in pursuit of large prey animals. We know that many monkeys and apes will eat meat whenever they get the chance and all we had to do was to increase that element in our lives and become the first pack-hunting primates – a kind of wolf-ape.

A Hagerhai hunting party in Papua New Guinea. Early in our evolutionary story our ape ancestors switched from fruit picking to hunting as a way of life. This change was to forge our human personality, making us more cooperative, more communicative, more dextrous and more intelligent.

A modern Innuit deer hunt. Hunting for survival today is rare, but can still be observed in remote corners of the globe. For most modern people the hunting phase of our evolution is over and food is more easily available. For them, it is necessary to find symbolic substitutes for the primeval chase.

Whether or not this is the simple way in which it happened, it is certainly true that we did end up, eventually, as a group-hunting primate. This hunting way of life changed us in several vitally important ways. Firstly, it made us more cooperative. We had to help one another if we were to succeed in the hunt. And this help had to be active, not passive.

Some people have argued that we were more likely to have begun as scavengers rather than hunters, as though this makes some major difference to our human story. But as scavengers, our ancestors must have been just as cooperative and determined if they were to drive other predators off their kills. In terms of changing the personality of a primate from ape to man, the scavenging/hunting debate is really of little interest. Being great opportunists, the chances are that we used our group strategies either to drive away other killers or to kill animals ourselves, according to the specific circumstances in which we happened to find ourselves at any one time. Our great strength was in our adaptability – a primate for all seasons.

It is hard for some people to accept the idea that by becoming meat-eaters we became more altruistic. But observe how chimpanzees feed. When they are engaged in eating fruits or nuts they are selfish. They do not share their food. There is no point in doing so. This applies to all herbivores. Each individual eats what he picks himself. But chimpanzees do share their food on the special occasions when they have managed to make a kill. If they have chased, caught and slaughtered a monkey, there is more meat than the killers themselves can swallow, so others get a portion. From these small beginnings, mutual aid and group cohesion can develop.

Secondly, our new hunting lifestyle made us more communicative. We needed to tell one another our intentions in some detail. From our ape grunts grew our human language.

Thirdly, we became more dextrous. We needed artificial weapons and tools to make up for the absence of sharp claws, great fangs and shearing teeth. We had to improve our manipulation of our new world, both literally and figuratively.

Having made our weapons, we had to improve our aiming ability when using them. Chimpanzees will throw sticks and stones at their enemies – predators such as leopards are bombarded in this way – but the aiming involved is rather vague and haphazard. In captivity, when tested in the laboratory, they show that they are capable of aiming with some accuracy but in the wild this manual skill is never refined. As serious hunters, we had to refine it. We had to develop a primeval accuracy that is today reflected in the modern archer's skill.

As athletes, chasing after swift prey on the tropical plains, the traditional evolutionary view suggests that we must have overheated. Those individuals with thinner coats of hair would have run faster and longer. Gradually our fur coats were discarded. During the cold of the night this created a problem. We became chilled. The answer was to develop a layer of adipose fat beneath our now naked skin. This warmed us when cold but did not interfere with our copious sweating when hot. It was the ideal combination.

Our exposed skins were doubtless dark enough to protect us from the ultraviolet rays of the sun, enabling us to hunt in the heat of the day as well as in the cool of the early morning or late evening. Much later, when we expanded our range to the sunless north, we became paler and paler, as our hides did their best to absorb any tiny traces of sunlight that were available.

That, in a nutshell, is the traditional story. But it fails to explain several strange features of our anatomy and behaviour. If we became pack hunters why did we not develop four-footed galloping? Monkeys and apes can scamper along on the ground much faster than a man can run. Becoming bipedal must have slowed us down greatly, especially in the early stages when we were in the process of changing our style of locomotion.

Also, if we lost our coat of fur as a cooling device, then why have the other plains killers, like the lion and the cheetah, the hunting dog and the hyena, remained hairy? Furthermore, why do the bodies of human females carry even less hair when they are less muscular and less athletic than the males? If they could not run so fast – and anyway were most of the time weighed down by babies – why did they need such naked cooling skins?

There seems no escaping the idea that something else, something odd, happened to us during the mysterious millennia of the Pliocene Gap. To date, only one serious suggestion has been put forward and it has met with considerable opposition. This is the aquatic theory of man's origin and it suggests that our ancestors passed through a water-living stage, when many of our modern features first appeared.

This theory has been criticized by the more entrenched traditionalists, who point out that it is entirely conjectural and there is no single shred of direct evidence to support it. What they fail to admit is that their own 'savannah hunting theory' is equally circumstantial.

The human species is amazingly at home in the water. It is a serious possibility that our ancestors went through an aquatic stage somewhere between four and seven million years ago, which would explain many of our peculiar features. Handled carefully, even newborn babies are capable of swimming without any training.

Its only merit is that it is simpler but since it fails to explain so many unique oddities of the human species, the alternative aquatic theory is, at the very least, worthy of serious scrutiny.

The theory first occurred to marine biologist Sir Alister Hardy in the summer of 1930 when he was leafing through a newly published volume by an anatomist who remarked that anyone 'who has repeatedly skinned both human subjects and any other members of the primates' will have noticed the layer of subcutaneous fat attached to the skin that is unique to man. He concluded that it 'is possibly related to apparent hair reduction; though it is difficult to see why, if no other factor is invoked, there should be such a basal difference between Man and the Chimpanzee'.

Alister Hardy guessed immediately what that 'other factor' must be. As a young man he had been at sea watching the early whalers at work and the great layers of blubber attached to the skin of the giant sea mammals had made a lasting impression on him. In a flash he knew what human body fat was – it was human blubber! But why on earth should we need blubber unless we had been through an aquatic stage in our evolution?

On another page of the anatomist's volume, Hardy came across a second clue. There were some drawings showing that the directions of the human hair-tracts are different from those of apes. The anatomist again declared ignorance, commenting that 'such differences can only be noted as human distinctions of uncertain diagnostic value'. But Hardy understood immediately: our special hair-tracts had evolved as streamlining when the human body was moving through the water. There seemed to be no other explanation as to why the directions of our hair-tracts should differ from those of apes in such a peculiar way.

It also occurred to him that our bipedal posture might have first started to evolve as a reaction to the new locomotory demands of our aquatic activities. Hardy decided, however, to await the discovery of fossil evidence to support his theory before publishing his thoughts on the subject. He kept them to himself for thirty years until, in 1960, when making a speech to a local subaqua club, he could not resist the temptation to mention his idea. To his dismay, his comments were picked up by journalists and appeared, completely garbled, in newspapers worldwide, forcing him to publish in a more serious form. As a professor of zoology he knew that he would be ridiculed for suggesting something so outlandish as an entirely new interpretation of human evolution. And indeed he was. But little by little, as the years have passed, the concept of an aquatic ape has been taken more seriously, until whole conferences have been held to discuss its merits.

Hardy's vision was of an early primate being driven onto offshore islands on what was then the east coast of Africa. Retreating there to escape predators, it established itself in small colonies. Once established, it began increasingly to adopt the lifestyle, as Hardy put it, of a 'tropical penguin'. The new-style body developed as an efficient swimming machine. Like penguins, these aquatic primates were originally more athletic in the water and more clumsy on land. The bipedal walking that we take for granted today would initially have been a grave disadvantage when ashore and could only have been nursed through its early stages in a peaceful environment such as Hardy's predator-free islands.

Hardy's theory explains many puzzling features of the human animal. In addition to our blubber and streamlined hair-tracts, it makes it easier to understand the following:

• We have more flexible spines than other apes, enabling us to swim more like otters than primates.

• We can weep copious tears, as can many other marine animals but no other primates.

• We have a sense of balance as good as a sealion's and much better than any other primate.

• We have lost the long, shaggy coat of fur that is typical of primates but not of marine animals. They always have short coats or no coats. This streamlining would improve our smooth passage through the water.

• We have partial webbing between our fingers and toes, again unlike any other primate. This webbing, although now only vestigial, is especially clear when the thumb is spread wide from the forefinger. We take this for granted, as a normal part of primate hand design, but if you examine the thumb of a chimpanzee, you will find that there the fold of webbing is missing. And most people are surprised to learn that anatomical records reveal that, even today, seven per cent of the world's population of humans still have webbed toes.

• We can swim with great athleticism, whereas the great apes cannot swim at all. Human swimming records include a non-stop swim of 168 hours, continuous water-treading lasting for 72 hours, a continuous swim lasting for 292 miles (470 kilometres) and an unaided dive to a depth of 262 feet (80 metres).

*As a primate species we have an unusually
flexible spine – typical of aquatic animals –
and we are capable of hunting fish using
only primitive weapons.*

*These small boys in Kenya's
Rift Valley can be seen catching
fish like otters, without the aid
of any weapons. They are living
today in the very region where
the human species evolved.
Could this have been our
preferred way of life several
million years ago?*

• We can hold our breath under water for as long as three and a half minutes. Furthermore, our exceptional voluntary breath control, quite beyond anything seen in other primates, would make it easier for us to start refining our primate grunts, leading eventually to talking and the evolution of speech. Such breath control would only be of major use, originally, in an aquatic environment.

• We have a 'diving reflex', like other marine mammals. This means that special nerve endings on our faces, around the mouth and nose, trigger this reflex only when the facial region is submerged in water. If we tread water, with our head out in the air, there is no diving reflex. But if we sink just our face in a bowl of water, while the whole of the rest of our body is in the dry air, the diving reflex is triggered. It automatically closes down the airway, reducing the risk of swallowing water, and it constricts the small air-passages in the lungs. At the same time the heart rate is slowed down to half speed and blood is shunted to the vital organs, protecting them from the effects of the temporary cessation of breathing. By contrast, if a chimpanzee or a gorilla found itself in water with its face below the surface, it would panic, its heart would race and it would quickly drown (as many zoos discovered to their cost when they first installed water-ditches around ape enclosures).

• We have a unique nose shape that shields the nostrils from water intake when we dive. No other primate has a nose of this type.

• Our newborn babies automatically hold their breath when placed under water and swim without fear if placed gently below the surface in a prone position.

• Above all, we have an unusual love of water for a primate and return to it in a hundred different ways. When we wish to give ourselves a special treat, we take a vacation at the seaside, on the ocean or floating in the coral reefs. We employ huge, modern machines costing millions to fly us to faraway places where we can enjoy the primeval pleasures of splashing about in rock pools. Even at home, one of the most soothing things we can do at the end of a stressful day is to lie back and relax in a hot bath. (Psychological studies have shown that for most people the reward of taking a hot bath is calming rather than cleansing.) This is not the behaviour of a typical, land-based primate that evolved solely on the dry plains.

A glance at Olympic swimmers in action, daring high-divers in Acapulco, cross-Channel swimmers, Japanese pearl-divers or adventurous scuba-divers makes one marvel at man's ability to flourish in an aquatic medium.

When assembled in this way, the evidence for an aquatic origin for our species certainly looks impressive. It is now up to field workers to locate hard evidence to support the theory, which will entail arduous searching for fossil remains along what were the African coastlines of the Pliocene period. Some of these coastlines have sunk, but others have become elevated, and it is there (most probably in the Danakil Mountains of East Africa) that the final answer may lie hidden.

If the traditionalists continue to reject this theory, fearing that it may disrupt their own, carefully presented scenario of the primeval 'plains hunter', they are being unnecessarily defensive. The two theories are far from incompatible. Indeed, they make a perfect combination, with the aquatic phase being a salutary baptism for our early forbears, before taking on the challenge of hunting the bigger game on the savannahs.

In fact it could be argued that, far from clashing, the two theories need one another. The aquatic ape had to come ashore eventually and transform itself into a mainland hunter. And the mainland hunter needed some unusual beginning to explain its unique form. Had we moved straight onto the hot savannahs from the forests, we would almost certainly have become intensely adapted to dry country living, yet this has not happened.

Consider the following human features: we have to drink more than any other land mammal; we sweat more than any other mammal; we die quickly if we overheat; we have dilute urine; and we produce moist dung. These five qualities contrast strongly with the water economy of typical savannah-living animals. They have responded to the hot, dry atmosphere by evolving special mechanisms for reducing water loss. The hunting dogs and big cats can suffer twice as much dehydration as we can before dying. Ten per cent dehydration kills humans but it takes twenty per cent to kill cats or dogs.

The excessive sweating of humans may be a good cooling device but it also uses up a huge amount of water – up to fifteen litres (over three gallons) a day under a tropical sun. This is not a loss that is typical of animals that have an ancient adaptation to hot, dry country. Also, a great deal of salt is lost in this sweat. For a marine ape, eating seafood, this would mean a valuable removal of excess salt but for a salt-starved savannah hunter it would create an additional problem.

Hot-country animals such as hunting dogs or camels are able to survive rises of body temperature to over forty degrees centigrade. These are levels that would kill any human being. Hot-country animals also have very concentrated urine compared with humans. Their dung is also much drier, containing only forty to fifty per cent water, compared with seventy-five per cent for humans. This means that they are able to rid themselves of waste matter with a far smaller loss of precious water.

Altogether these features mean that we are strangely reckless with our water losses for an animal that is supposed to have specialized, from an early stage, as an occupant of the baking African savannahs. It seems much more likely that we originally stayed close to water supplies, including fresh water, until we had developed many of our more advanced characteristics. Only then were we ready to venture out on the hunting plains and take our chances alongside the specialized killers already there. This readiness would increase considerably the likelihood that we went through an aquatic 'apprenticeship', basing ourselves in wet regions where we could enjoy both fresh and sea water – presumably somewhere near the mouths of rivers.

How does this combined aquatic-to-savannah scenario relate to human diet? Before the aquatic phase, our remote ancestors must have followed the usual primate feeding pattern of consuming a wide variety of plant foods – fruits, nuts, berries, roots and succulent stems – with a crucial supplement of animal foods such as termites, birds' eggs, nestlings and the occasional kill. If they then made the shift to the seashore and began to collect and consume large quantities of seafood – switching from 'fruits of the forest' to '*fruits de mer*' – they would have greatly increased their animal protein intake without having to make any great changes in food preparation. If they were skilful at cracking open nuts, this could easily be applied to opening shellfish.

Gradually becoming bolder and plunging deeper into the sea to obtain these nutritious new foods, it is easy to see how our ancestors could have become increasingly aquatic. An abundance of pebbles would have offered them a ready supply of simple tools for smashing the harder shells and out of this activity more elaborate tool use would have grown. A pebble accidentally split into a sharp-edged flint would make the first knife. From there it was only a small step to the first spearhead and fish hunting could then be added to the collection of shellfish.

It is possible that their rich and varied new diet helped considerably in the evolution of a larger brain and greater intelligence. Herbivorous diets are always nutritionally inferior to carnivorous ones and the gradual change in feeding behaviour could have enabled our ancestors to make a major leap forward.

Thriving in this new environment, and with a much more highly developed taste for animal foods, it is not hard to imagine our ancient ancestors becoming more ambitious and returning to the mainland, ready now to outwit the land-based predators. Once there, they could expand their menu to include meat from a variety of terrestrial animals. Their taste for animal prey acquired in the shallows could now be applied to the bigger game on the plains. And with their greater intelligence they could organize their lives so that they always had a suitably generous supply of drinking water. From this point onward, the story of our evolution reverts to the traditional savannah scenario.

When the sea ape became a hunting ape, several important new developments occurred. The arduous, cooperative hunt for large prey meant that females with babies were at risk. The whole group could not attack together. A division of labour was needed, with the males becoming more muscular and athletic and slightly more specialized for the chase.

If they could not accompany the male hunters, the females with young and the older members of the group had to be left somewhere in safety. Furthermore, this had to be a known site, so that the males could return there after their kill, to share the food. It meant that this pioneering primate species had to develop the new idea of a fixed 'home base'.

In fact, the new 'Hunting Ape' had to behave more like a territorial wolf pack than a wandering monkey troop. Settlements had to be established. This in turn led to a new problem – vulnerability. The non-hunting members of the group were 'sitting targets' for a variety of predators. The home base needed some sort of protection. Shelters had to be built. Simple huts were made. A territorial ape was in the making.

This changed the social life of our ancestors dramatically. The division of labour became greater. While the males became ever more efficient hunters, the females became more specialized as food-gatherers. Pair bonds developed that kept individual females emotionally close to their physically distant males. The nuclear family became the basic unit of the group.

Hygiene became more important because of the re-use of home-base dwellings. We became the only one of the 193 species of monkeys and apes to have fleas. In fact we have our own species of flea. Fleas can only go through their life-cycle if their host animal lives in a repeatedly inhabited den or lair. This alone is proof that we did become lair dwellers from a very early stage in our human story. Nomads come much later and are not as basic in their way of life as some people seem to think.

To sum up the human story so far: our ancestors started out as fruit-picking tree dwellers, which (probably) became seafood-collecting shore dwellers, which eventually became carnivorous savannah dwellers. In the process we changed our primate habits and ceased in many ways to behave like our ape relatives. The change was not total, however. Some of our older patterns survived but they were joined by our newer ones. In our behaviour we became a kind of hybrid, part primate and part carnivore, part ape and part wolf, part fruit picker and part hunter. This double character has stayed with us to this day and there is an undercurrent of two primal forces at work in our modern lifestyles, especially where our feeding behaviour is concerned.

To understand this it is necessary to take a closer look at the way a cooperative hunt takes place and at the patterns of behaviour it involves. Because of their comparatively puny bodies, men must use their wits to survive. They must use their intelligence to prepare artificial weapons to make up for their lack of fangs and claws. These weapons must be constructed, cared for, cleaned and made ready for the hunt.

Next, a strategy must be agreed. This involves precise communication and it is no exaggeration to say that planning the hunt was probably the first great survival pressure out of which human language grew. We had to give names to our prey and sit together and plan our method of attacking them.

The earliest clothing was probably no more than some kind of belt or strap for carrying basic hunting equipment and perhaps some sort of cover to protect the male genitals from damage. Once the hunt was under way, there was the need for prolonged trekking and ultimately, if necessary, fast running. The chase became an essential part of male existence and required athleticism, stamina and a temperament that encouraged persistence.

This last point was all important. Fruit picking does not require prolonged concentration or long-distance goals. Hunting does, and it changed us dramatically. In place of the selfish, minute-by-minute lifestyle of the typical herbivore or fruit picker, the hunting ape developed the ability to concentrate for long periods of time on an organized project. Group-related, prolonged, undivided attention of this kind was to prove to be one of mankind's greatest debts to the primeval hunt.

Once the prey had been reached or cornered, it had to be killed and this involves aiming. We had to become masters of this special skill. We also had to become brave. Monkeys are rather timid creatures. Even the great apes are shy and retiring by nature. Our ancestors had to become bold, if we were to make a living out of killing large prey that could easily become dangerous when driven to extreme measures. We had to take risks and be prepared to expose ourselves to considerable dangers. This would have applied just as much on the occasions when we were scavenging, because we would have had to use all our courage to drive lions or other predators off their kills.

Next, we had to be skilful at carrying, skinning and cutting up the carcass of our prey. For this we needed further cooperation between the members of the group and an improvement in our tool-making.

Finally, we had to evolve a more sharing mentality. If the group was to survive and breed, we had to take a leaf out of the book of predators such as wolves and hunting dogs, and give part of our kill to the younger, older or weaker members of the group. The hunt made us more altruistic. It also gave us the special pleasure of feasting, something denied the herbivorous monkey. The high quality of the food devoured on these occasions enabled us to pursue other aspects of social life during the rest of the day. As hunters, we changed our whole rhythm of feeding.

That was the new way of life that was to lead ultimately to … us. And if we go out and about to make observations on the way we behave today, it soon becomes clear that many of our primeval, tribal hunting patterns are still with us, lightly disguised.

A few genuine hunts still take place, reminding us of the original pattern. But for the vast majority of human beings today, the acquisition of food is easy. The agricultural revolution has seen to that. We do not need to set out armed with special weapons, undertake a long chase and involve ourselves in dangerous struggles with powerful animals in order to bring home the joint from the local supermarket. We are very tame hunters today. So what has happened to all those old hunting urges? How does modern man fulfil the demands of his ancient heritage?

Hunting substitutes take many forms. Some 'hunters' travel on long journeys to take 'shots' with a camera; others spend hours searching for hidden treasure; still others compete furiously to bring home a symbolic prey in the form of a sporting trophy.

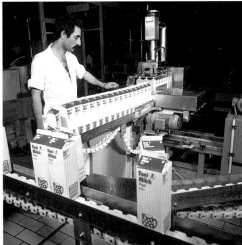

Today, working takes the place of hunting. The workplace has become a symbolic hunting ground. Young males try to make a 'killing' in the city to 'bring home the bacon' for their families.

For some, the workplace lacks the excitement of the hunt. The tasks are monotonously repetitive. For these individuals a symbolic hunt must be found elsewhere, in their leisure time, through sport and other competitive pastimes.

The answer is that there are many ways, some ordinary, some wonderful and some hideous. Because the original survival hunt has all but disappeared, we are now free to replace it with whatever symbolic substitution takes our fancy, just so long as it contains some, or all, of the same basic elements.

Today, for most people, 'going to work' is the major substitute for hunting. For the lucky ones, the nature of their daily work is sufficiently close to the pattern of the primeval hunt to be satisfying. The businessman setting off in the morning, eager to make a 'killing' in the city, with his schemes and strategies, his team tactics and his targets, his immediate aims and his long-term goals, hoping to confirm a contract or close a deal, and eventually to 'bring home the bacon' – he is the fulfilled pseudo-hunter of modern times.

But for many other people, their work is so boringly repetitive that it provides little of the excitement or challenge of the hunt and is a poor substitute for it. If we were descendants of cud-chewing herbivores, this would not matter but we are not, and it does. People with boring work become restless and frustrated. They have to find other outlets for their 'hunter's brain'. Some of these outlets are creative. Others can be highly destructive.

For many individuals, a lack of 'job satisfaction' – which can usually be traced to a lack of potential for symbolic hunting – is made tolerable by the development of some kind of hobby or private passion. During leisure hours the frustrated hunter indulges in activities which, although of little importance in themselves, provide him with a scenario that offers many of the elements of the primeval chase. Such 'pursuits' (even this name is revealing) include collecting, gambling, travelling and all forms of competitive games and sports.

In collecting, humans set themselves more or less arbitrary tasks and then spend years tracking down exciting new items to add to their assembly of objects. The special quality of every collection is that it must be based on a clearly defined category. That category must not be too narrow or too wide. Within it there must be enough variety to add interest; nobody collects endless examples of identical objects. But equally there must not be too much variety or the hunt for new examples will become too easy.

The range of objects collected by this type of symbolic hunter is extraordinary – everything from snuff-boxes to steam engines, from autographs to aeroplanes, from postage stamps to porcelain. The symbolic equation is simple enough: the next object to be added to the collection becomes the 'prey'. Like true, live prey, it is difficult to find and frequently (financially) dangerous to obtain. So there has to be careful planning, prolonged searching, stealthy tactics (bargaining) and then the joy of the final kill – the purchase of the object. It is then carried home in triumph and added to the collection, where the new owner can 'feast' his eyes upon it.

So powerful is this form of symbolic hunting that it can easily become an obsession. It can take over an individual's life to the point where little else matters and he lives only for the moment that he can return to his beloved collection, study it and analyse it, and then set off on yet another hunting trip.

Gambling can become equally addictive. Here the thrill is essentially in risk taking. The primeval hunt involved great potential danger and if life becomes too boringly safe and mundane, then some kind of hazard must be put back into it, even if it means inventing one, as in a wager or a bet. For the gambler to make a successful 'killing' he must use all his skills – at the card table or the race track – to beat the system. He must gamble enough money to hurt if he loses and bring joy if he wins. A trivial sum would not provide the 'danger' he seeks.

For many other would-be hunters, some kind of 'unnecessary travelling' provides an attractive alternative. The rambler, the camper, the trekker, the explorer and the tourist all engage in what could be called 'inquisitive locomotion'. More ritualized forms of travel, such as racing, sailing, riding and flying, are also strong favourites for filling the spare time of the thwarted hunter that is modern man. All such pursuits provide the search and chase elements of the hunt that are missing from otherwise house-bound, office-bound and factory-bound lives.

Many games and sports also provide elements of the chase. Some offer the chance to aim at a symbolic prey – be it the bull's eye of a target, the pocket of a pool table or the goal mouth of a football pitch. There is hardly any sport on earth that does not offer a symbolic chase, or a symbolic kill, or both. And with most of our major sporting events there are trophies to be won – cups, plaques, statues and medals – which we carry home in triumph. These glistening, glittering prizes symbolize for the modern pseudo-hunters the spoils to be brought back to the home base as the final climax of the long struggle. They may be inedible but they are so hard-earned that their symbolic significance over-shadows their uselessness.

The way we feed still bears the hallmarks of our hunting past. We continue to enjoy great celebratory feasts and we invent a whole variety of special occasions that allow us to re-create, unconsciously, the primeval tribal sharing of the hunters' kill.

Even our day-to-day meals reflect our carnivorous evolution. Animals that eat plants – stems, leaves, fruits, nuts and roots – do not have spaced out 'meals'. They munch away all day with almost non-stop snacks. Because of the low nutritional quality of their food they must eat a great deal of it and this involves them in hour after hour of repetitive biting and chewing. A giraffe, for example, feeds for 12 out of every 24 hours, devouring 143 pounds (65 kilos) of vegetation each day of its life.

Gorillas feed throughout most of the morning and then, after a midday rest, throughout most of the afternoon as well. They have never been observed to share their food and there is little or no communication during the endless eating. The only noises to be heard are an occasional grunt or belch, the snapping of twigs and a little lip smacking. Although the group stays together as the animals move through the forest, feeding is essentially an individual activity.

This contrasts strongly with the behaviour of a pack-hunting carnivore, where feeding is a major social event. We, with our double background of primate turned 'carnivore', show both types of feeding behaviour. Under normal circumstances, we eat three social meals each day but we also enjoy small snacks in between these main events. It is significant that we hardly ever eat meat when we are snacking. Meat is confined to the main social events, which represent the carnivorous half of our inheritance. Our snacks are nearly always sweet-tasting – such as biscuits, chocolates, candies, soft drinks, sweetened tea or coffee. They reflect our primeval interest in ripe, sweetened fruits and berries.

Our snacks are often taken individually, independent of the feeding activities of others, while our main meals are nearly always eaten in groups – either in family units in the home or in 'tribal eating places' such as restaurants or cafés. We are happy enough to nibble our snacks in solitary splendour but we feel a primeval need for company when eating a full meal. These two feeding modes again reflect our ancient ancestry – the independent snack-eater versus the sociable feaster, the human primate versus the human 'carnivore'.

Our dual personality, where feeding is concerned, has been one of our great strengths. As omnivores, we have proved amazingly adaptable. Although, nutritionally, we need a balanced mixture of 'meat and veg' to thrive, we are capable of tipping the balance strongly in either direction. We can survive on an almost entirely vegetable diet or an almost entirely meat diet. Neither extreme is ideal for the human stomach but such is our flexibility that we can make do with almost any combination.

If this is the case, then why should there be twenty million human deaths every year from nutritional deprivation? The answer lies in the mixed blessing of the agricultural revolution. Agriculture led to a food surplus that enabled human populations to increase rapidly. But it also led to most of these populations relying on one major, staple crop – rice, wheat, corn, millet or manioc. In affluent times this created no problem because there would also be enough meat to go around. But in times of hardship, when meat became scarce, the monotonous new diet of the deprived poor fell far short of what the human body required. This was especially true in the cases of infants, growing children and pregnant or lactating women. Growing children have four times the adult need for animal protein and it was inevitably they who suffered most.

To argue that, as primates, we should be able to fall back on a herbivorous or vegetable diet without any damage to ourselves is to miss the point. The millions suffering from malnutrition in the modern world are victims of a narrow, restricted vegetable diet. Monkeys and apes typically eat a huge range of plant foods and they always take a few animal supplements – even if those are no more than insects and eggs. Theirs is a wonderfully varied diet. Third World poverty does not offer that variety.

Secondly, we appear to have changed genetically during the course of our evolution, to a point where we need meat to keep us healthy. Our digestive system has been modified in such a way that we can now only obtain the proper balance of the eight essential amino acids we require if they come from animal protein. It is true that these amino acids can also be obtained from plant foods but not all together and not in the correct balance. To re-create this balance requires deft culinary juggling that is (at present, as in the past) quite beyond the starving millions of much of the world.

We must accept that a million years of hunting has genetically changed the diet of our species and that ten thousand years of crop feeding has not been long enough to modify it a second time. If, for philosophical reasons, we wish to become predominantly vegetarian, we must face up to this fact and consider carefully whether we are depriving our children

We are the greatest omnivores on the planet. We eat almost anything. Our diet is typified by the vast variety of food that is available and by our elaborate cuisines which offer endless variations of taste and texture. This is the double legacy we enjoy from our ancient 'hunting ape' ancestors and our even more ancient fruit-picking primate ancestors.

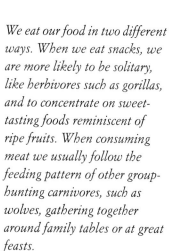

We eat our food in two different ways. When we eat snacks, we are more likely to be solitary, like herbivores such as gorillas, and to concentrate on sweet-tasting foods reminiscent of ripe fruits. When consuming meat we usually follow the feeding pattern of other group-hunting carnivores, such as wolves, gathering together around family tables or at great feasts.

*We evolved as a 'feast or famine' species with an uncertain food supply. As a result we developed bodies that, during times of feasting, store body fat for the famine days to come. If, as a consequence of modern affluence, we enjoy, not feast/famine but feast/feast, we are liable to become fatter and fatter. The body stores fat for bad days that never come. This is why modern dieting methods seldom work; as soon as we have imposed an artificial famine on our bodies they rebel.*

of their extremely high protein demands. And we must also ensure that our vegetable foods are as varied and balanced as possible. In addition, we must accept that it is vital to take at least a small amount of animal food, even if it is only as a minor supplement.

In other words, if, as a matter of principle, we wish to abandon the spoils of the primeval hunt and restrict ourselves entirely to symbolic 'kills', we must do so with great care and culinary skill, always bearing in mind the remarkably mixed diet of the 'fruit-picking monkeys'.

While the poverty-stricken parts of the world face starvation, the affluent West has quite another problem: it is overweight. Obesity has become a major health hazard among the wealthy nations and a thousand different food regimes have been invented to cure it. Why should this be? Wild animals do not seem to suffer from this problem, even when the living is good and food is plentiful. There are no chubby cheetahs or podgy pumas, no tubby tigers or stout stoats. What is it about us that, when we eat well, causes us to grow so fat?

The answer lies again in our hunting past. As long as our remote ancestors stayed in the forests or on the sea-shores, the food supply was fairly regular but as soon as they switched to hunting large prey, the situation changed. For a million years, as they spread out across the globe, probing relentlessly into new environments, they must have faced the risks of an uncertain food supply. If, as a result, they suffered a 'feast or famine' mode of existence, it would have been a great advantage to have some sort of emergency food supply. Today we have larders and refrigerators but they had to rely on something more biological. The answer was the human equivalent of the camel's hump: body fat. The difference, however, was that with us the fat was distributed all over the body. If we had already obtained a general layer of blubber from our aquatic days, we had the perfect base on which to build. By increasing that layer when food was plentiful, we could survive through the 'lean' years by literally 'living on our fat'.

If we changed genetically in relation to this 'feast or famine' lifestyle, it would be quite natural for us to 'overeat' in affluent times, grow fat, and then thin down again when times were hard. It follows of course that if, instead of alternating good and bad times, we experience good and good times, we will keep on adding 'security fat' but never losing it. This is precisely why 'crash diets' nearly always fail. During the voluntary starvation period of our carefully designed 'diets', our genes tell us 'get ready to gorge again'. As time passes, the genetic message grows stronger, until it becomes irresistible. The rigid diet is followed by a glorious binge or, at the very least, a return to the old, generous eating habits. In this way we artificially re-create, in modern terms, the age-old feast and famine routine.

It is clear that this personal food storage system became particularly important when our ancestors spread to more northern regions. There, the migrating herds of prey animals and the dramatic seasonal changes would have meant bigger feasts and bigger famines.

*The Willendorf Venus. This ancient figurine, fashioned twenty-four thousand years ago, shows that the storage of body fat was a celebrated achievement in the Old Stone Age when risk of famine was ever-present.*

We can see the results of this in the extraordinary obesity of the prehistoric figurines of women which have been discovered in recent years. These so-called 'Venus Figures' show huge buttocks and wide hips, and should really be renamed the 'Goddesses of the Feast', celebrating, as they must surely have done, the affluent periods when there was gorging and fattening against the hard times ahead. Perhaps they were carried during the lean periods to encourage, by magic, the return of the feasting days.

These little prehistoric figurines are found at sites scattered across Europe, the Middle East and the more northerly regions of Asia. Later, they are replaced by more slender, graceful shapes. The reason for the change is not hard to find. Increasingly efficient, man-made food storage techniques have arrived on the scene. Body fat storage is no longer so important.

If the primeval hunter inside us can find creative symbolic outlets through challenging work and absorbing leisure pursuits, through sports and games, and also in mealtime gatherings, then in theory all should be well. The ancient human energy to pursue prey can now be channelled into the hunt for more abstract goals and into the pursuit of excellence. Unfortunately, that same energy can all too easily be channelled into destructive outlets.

Every day we are bombarded with news of outbreaks of human violence. All such cases are lumped together in the popular mind as examples of human aggression. This shows a profound misunderstanding of the nature of animal aggression.

Aggression, in the true sense, is the assertive settling of disputes between individuals. In the animal world this is nearly always achieved by display, by threat and by counter-threat. It is rare to see blood flow during these hostile encounters. Animal aggression is common but all-out animal fighting is extremely rare. On those occasions when they do come to blows, the fights themselves are usually stylized. Animals pull their punches. In fact it is true to say that, for animals, violence is the failure of aggression.

In the human sphere, true aggression – as distinct from violence – is also common. Arguments between neighbours, family tiffs, altercations between motorists and other such disputes are typical examples of 'animal aggression', where assertiveness takes the form of displays and counter-displays, until the argument is settled.

A great deal of modern human violence is not true animal aggression but perverted hunting in which the victim becomes a substitute prey. The victim of the lynch mob is not involved in a personal dispute, and there is no personal dispute between the pilot of the rocket-carrying aircraft and the tiny speck on the ground which is his target.

For humans, the most common form of aggressive display is verbal abuse. This may be intensely hostile but no spoken word has ever drawn blood. Alternatively, we have a magnificent range of hostile facial expressions and body postures to deploy against our rivals, again without spilling their blood. Even if we are driven to the rare extreme of a physical encounter, the fighting is usually no more than a few slaps and blows that leave little more than a black eye or a bruised cheek.

Quite distinct from these commonplace occurrences are the seriously violent incidents. These usually have little to do with true aggression. Whether they are cases of mugging, where a gang beats up a stranger, or terrorism, where a group commits an atrocity against innocent bystanders, or full-blown warfare, they all belong to a completely different category of behaviour. These are not cases of aggression, they are examples of symbolic hunting turned sour.

The key difference is in the nature of the victim. True aggression involves disputes between individual rivals. The primary function of the aggressive acts is to intimidate and dominate these rivals. Where violent symbolic hunting is concerned, the victim is depersonalized and becomes, not the rival, but the 'prey'.

Human warfare is our most destructive form of symbolic hunting. If there is any true aggression involved it is restricted purely to the rival leaders, who are genuinely concerned with changing their status relations. But for the ordinary fighting men at the front, aggression is rarely involved. Instead, what we witness is a reciprocal pseudo-hunt. Groups of men enter the fray with complete strangers in their sights. They have no personal knowledge whatever of the enemy troops, who, if they are visible at all, appear as no more than tiny, impersonal specks in the distance. They are killed, not through anger or personal rivalry, but through the need of each fighting man to support his 'buddies'. Loyalty to the regiment, to the cause or to the nation is always the most important aspect of wartime violence.

In other words, the primeval hunting pack is re-created as a group of warriors and the motivation of its members is more to do with mutual aid than with anything else. The enemy soldiers are not people, they are prey. They are to be picked off, impersonally, without any reference to their emotional states, their moods or their feelings. The fact that they wear different uniforms helps to make them seem to belong to another species.

Corrupting our hunting urges in this way is only easy when our daily lives do not give us more positive, creative ways of expressing ourselves. Unfortunately, in every modern society there are sufficient young males who do not find enough fulfilment in creative hunting substitutes and who are always available for the destructive alternatives.

Our method of dealing with such people, when their violence fails, is to make them civilian prisoners or prisoners of war. This procedure amounts to imposing on them a lifestyle even more remote from their primeval hunting heritage than the one that drove them to be violent in the first place. This is a dilemma that, as yet, we have not begun to solve.

None of this was such a problem back in the days when we lived in small tribal groups. It is our amazing success story as an animal species that has created our modern headaches. To understand how that has come about it is necessary to trace the rise of the 'urban ape'.

# 3

# *The Human Zoo*

It took more than a million years for our ancestors to evolve from fruit-picking apes to meat-eating humans. In that long journey through time, we gradually became set in a new mould – the tribal hunter. The tribes were small, probably each with fewer than a hundred individuals. The tribal settlement became established as the centre of human social life. It was the home base to which the hunters could return with their spoils. Village life had begun.

Then, about ten thousand years ago, this ancient pattern underwent a major change – farming replaced hunting. Food was stored. A food surplus was available and the human tribes began to swell. Villages became towns and towns became cities. In a mere hundred centuries we progressed from mud huts to skyscrapers, in a breathless rush towards some imagined technological paradise.

In certain ways our great cities did indeed become a paradise on earth, compared with the primeval settlements of ancient times. They gave us creature comforts and freedoms of many kinds – advantages beyond the wildest dreams of our early ancestors. But there was a price to pay. With each advance, our human populations grew. With every success, we became more overcrowded. As the quality of life increased, so did the quantity of human bodies. The tiny tribes of our prehistoric forbears enjoyed the open spaces of vast hunting grounds, stretching for miles in all directions, as far as the eye could see. It has been calculated that each primeval tribesman had one hundred thousand times more living space than the modern city-dweller.

So, to gain the rewards of civilization, the new citizen was forced to live in an environment totally unlike the one in which the human species evolved. It was a paradise full of stress. As a result, the city became a theatre of contrasts, modern comforts sharing the stage with unbearable tensions. New kinds of violence erupted. The stimulating creativity of the metropolis acquired a supporting case of crime, madness, cruelty and despair. The simple tribesman had become a civilized super-tribesman with a problem.

Viewing the savagery of the city, some writers referred to it as a concrete jungle. But

The city is not a concrete jungle it is a human zoo. City-dwellers suffer from many of the problems and disorders displayed by zoo animals.

jungles are not like that. In one way or another, the violence in the city all stems from abnormal overcrowding and jungles are not overcrowded. It is the kind of violence one sees not in a jungle but in an old-fashioned zoo.

That is why, when I came to write a sequel to *The Naked Ape*, dealing with modern city life, I called it *The Human Zoo*. For some years I had been studying the way in which captive animals behaved when crowded into small cages and I decided to compare that with the way city-dwellers reacted to their cramped urban environment. The parallels were remarkable and gave me some new insights into the nature of human aggression.

The first question I asked myself was: how does the modern super-tribe differ from the primeval tribal group? It is bigger, of course, but what does that mean to the individual? The answer can be summed up in a single word: strangers.

In the primeval tribe of between 80 and 120 people, everyone knew everyone else. There were no strangers in the group. If a few strangers from outside the group did arrive one day, they would arouse intense curiosity and would quickly become known personally and then cease to be strangers.

But what if there are a million strangers all around you in the city? Getting to know them personally is an impossibility. How do you react then? The answer is that you set up your own small, personal tribe from within the teeming masses of the city population and the rest you treat as non-people. You pretend they are not there. You avoid eye contact, you look away from them, you eliminate any greeting or social exchange. You treat them like trees in a forest. In the busy streets you develop human traffic skills of amazing dexterity. In crowded buses, trains and elevators you acquire a blank stare. You have eyes only for those you know. This enables you to enjoy the varied delights of the big city while mentally re-creating a personal tribal existence.

This adaptation to a life surrounded by strangers has some unflattering side-effects. It can make city-dwellers appear callous and uncaring, when in reality all they are trying to do is keep their tribal sanity in the face of constant stranger-bombardment. Take, for example, the case of the collapsed citizen. If someone is taken ill and falls to the ground on the sidewalk of a busy street, how do passers-by react?

We tested this in New York by asking someone to feign a collapse and lie still. As we suspected, people ignored the prostrate figure. They walked around it, stepped over it and generally avoided it as best they could. Most passers-by simply pretended that it was not there. A few peered closely at it and then walked on. It was a full five minutes before anyone offered a helping hand.

By contrast, a similar collapse in a small village produced an immediate response. In the small community, even a stranger is offered aid and treated as a person rather than a non-person. For village-dwellers, the anti-stranger defence mechanism has not been activated.

This difference reveals the extent to which the natural tribal urge to cooperate has to be suppressed in the urban environment. As the number of strangers mounts, the helpfulness fades. The urge to greet the individual encountered walking down the street, the urge to assist someone across the road, the urge to respond to a beggar's outstretched hand, all these natural feelings become atrophied in the artificial profusion of the metropolis. The numbers are so huge that the individual has no option.

Human cities have been likened to ant hills or termite colonies but the similarity is entirely superficial. About the only thing they have in common is the presence of the teeming masses of individuals. Ants and termites are not tribal animals. They have evolved as colonial species over millions of years. But the human city, when you look a little closer, is not a natural colony. It is an artificial aggregation, a complex network of interlocking and overlapping tribes. Examine the phone book or address book of any city-dweller and there you will find their true tribal group – the names and addresses of those people known at a personal level: friends, colleagues, relatives. For most of us, the numbers of personal acquaintances are remarkably similar to the numbers of humans that occupied the tribes of our ancient ancestors.

The pious platitudes of priests and politicians suggest that we should love all men equally, that we should treat every stranger as our brother. Biologically, we are simply not programmed to act that way. Biologically, we are a tribal species and will always give preference to the members of our own tribe. This may be an unpalatable truth but it is better to be honest about it if we are to handle its consequences well. If we act as though this tribal bias does not exist, then it will come back to haunt us in its worst forms. If we accept it, then we can try to tame it.

When all goes well, the way we tame it is to develop a formal system of impersonal courtesies that mimic genuine friendship. We call this system 'good manners' or 'etiquette'.

In the city we are surrounded by strangers and always avoid eye contact with them in public places. In this way we manage to remain tribal animals even in the greatest urban centres, with just a small number of close friends and relations as the known members of our personal group.

The impersonal nature of relationships in great urban centres is personified by the observation that if a body lies collapsed on a city street it is ignored. By contrast, if someone collapses in a village street, help is immediately forthcoming.

The paradox of the crowd. In the midst of the teeming city masses the individual becomes emotionally isolated. Unable to make personal contact with those around him, he turns them mentally into non-persons and walks through them as if they are trees in a forest.

The human animal evolved as an actively cooperative species. Small tribes could only survive if everyone helped everyone else. But in the impersonal, super-tribal atmosphere of the modern city, this natural human quality is rapidly eroded.

It enables us to mix with strangers with the minimum of friction. It means that when the interwoven tribes come into contact and rub against one another in social contexts, they can conduct themselves in a peaceful, amicable way.

The basis of this 'good behaviour' is reciprocal altruism. There is an unspoken contract between the urban strangers: 'You scratch my back and I will scratch yours'. Children take some time to learn this system and parents can frequently be overheard telling them to 'behave themselves'. This is a curious use of the word 'behave'. What the instruction really means is 'behave towards strangers as though they are friends'. At first, children find this a hard convention to obey but by the time they are young adults they are usually ready to accept the lie and play the social game.

One thing they soon discover is that, when disputes occur, the rules are not always the same. Arguments between true friends (or loved ones) can be outspoken and uninhibited without destroying the relationship. The mutual understanding that a strong bond exists between the individuals concerned permits a freedom of expression that is missing in the formal world of polite etiquette. There, a single rude comment may be enough to wreck the fragile and artificial peace. In the world of 'correct behaviour' the participants must walk on egg shells and sometimes the strain is too great. They momentarily lose control and the carefully nurtured façade collapses.

It has often been said that 'the law forbids men to do only what their instincts incline them to do'. If this is true, then the human animal must by nature be a cheating, thieving, torturing rapist. But I think not. The image of the primeval brute beating his companions over the head with a large club and dragging his female off to a cave by her hair is a cartoonist's fiction. There is no way in which we could have successfully evolved as an actively cooperative hunting species if we had lived like that. To have thrived as we must have done in those early days, to spread all over the globe, we must have been, biologically, a remarkably peaceful, restrained and helpful animal.

This sounds odd – so different from the picture most of us have of primitive human existence – but there is no escaping it. A great deal of the confusion seems to have arisen because people often fail to make a distinction between predatory and aggressive behaviour. When, in *The Naked Ape*, I spoke of our early ancestors as 'killer apes', I was referring to their feeding behaviour, not their behaviour towards one another. Despite this I was often misquoted as saying that mankind had an irrepressibly aggressive nature and was inherently violent. Nothing could be further from the truth.

The fact is that the more predatory a species becomes, the more restrained it must be in the use of its killing weapons on members of its own kind. Wolves, like men, are so efficient at killing deer that they must show powerful inhibitions when tempted to fight one another. They still engage in disputes over leadership, of course, but these disputes are settled by rituals and threat displays, rather than by tearing at one another's throats. Wolves could do one another such terrible damage in an all-out fight that even the winners would risk serious injury and would then be unable to hunt. So a really violent wolf species would soon become extinct. A successful wolf species would be one that sorted out its pack relationships without coming to blows. And that is the species that exists today. In the phrase 'Nature red in tooth and claw', the word 'red' refers to the blood of prey, not to that of rivals.

It is the same with human beings. When we developed our capacity to kill prey we had to make sure that we did not use our lethal abilities on one another. Like wolves, we evolved an improved system of submissive actions and appeasement displays that could be used to switch off the aggression of dominant animals. In other words, we acquired the biological equivalent of 'waving a white flag' or 'throwing in the towel'. We used body language instead of brute force. We replaced the action of sticking a dagger in someone with 'looking daggers' at them. In personal disputes the glance replaced the lance.

So how *do* we explain all the violence and mayhem in modern society? Basically, the answer is that the law does not forbid men to do what their instincts incline them to do but what their unnatural urban environment drives them to do.

To understand any form of human behaviour, the best way is to observe it at first hand. When someone is mugged in the street we immediately think of two things: helping the victim and catching the criminal. But why did this event occur? What did the victim represent to the attacker? The answer is that, being a stranger, he or she was a non-person. Not belonging to the personal tribe of the attacker, the victim was little more than a prey animal, a source of food. Not a direct source of food, of course, but a source of money which could be stolen to buy food. The attacker's pound of flesh is his victim's wallet.

*In personal disputes we still show the typically inhibited aggression seen in other animals. We argue and we threaten, we cower and we appease, but we rarely draw blood. We settle our differences with displays rather than physical violence.*

Mugging is not personal aggression, then. It is merely the exploitation of a local food source. There is a whole community – almost a tribe in itself – of criminals who would be repelled at the idea of hurting a friend or stealing from a relative. They are the thieves and burglars, the house-breakers and con men. They may sometimes use a degree of violence but only as much as is needed to help their basic goal of pseudo-hunting.

There is a second basic type of crime in modern cities, with a completely different character. This is violence for the sake of violence. Here the criminal wants to hurt – to abuse, defile, stab, beat, rape, torture and murder. The goals range from mere humiliation to the total destruction of another individual. This type of crime is not limited solely to strangers. It is redirected aggression and it can strike anywhere. Nobody who is weak or vulnerable is immune from it, regardless of whether they are inside the attacker's tribe or family, or outside it.

Most human violence is of this type and is caused by the enormous pressures that the urban world imposes upon its modern tribesmen. Only the most dominant individuals can avoid it. Their feeling of personal power gives them all the status satisfaction they

need. If they ever resort to violence it is purely for practical reasons and is dealt with in a matter-of-fact manner.

The weaker members of the urban super-tribe – and there are so many of them – suffer varying degrees of subordination. The great weight of the super-tribal machine squashes them to the bottom of the pile, where they lose face, are robbed of self-esteem and start to harbour anger and feelings of revenge. Too cowardly to attack the powerful source of their agony, they turn to weaker victims, substitutes on which they can vent their spleen.

The most common victims of this redirected aggression are women, children and animals. Wife beaters, rapists, child abusers and animal torturers belong to this category. So too do the vandals who take out their anger not on living beings but on inanimate objects, in orgies of wanton destruction. We often hear it said that the actions of all these criminals are meaningless and inexplicable but when we say this we are forgetting that they are carried out by social weaklings and failures who can find no other way of expressing their reaction to the unnaturally magnified urban competition. As acts of indirect revenge they do have meaning and they are explicable.

For many of these violent criminals, the damage is done in childhood and is difficult to eradicate. Reaction to abuse at a tender age goes underground and simmers there, waiting to erupt years later. As a result, predicting moments when redirected violence will occur is not easy.

These two flaws in the urban environment – stranger attack and redirected aggression – are a result of the huge size of the urban super-tribe. How do we set about protecting ourselves from this?

One of the most basic ways in which animals reduce aggression is to form territories. These are defended spaces in which the territory-owners are strong and intruders are weak. By keeping to separate patches, everyone has a share of the environment. Each territory provides its owners with a spatially limited form of dominance, making it possible for them to respect the territories of others.

This shared dominance is well suited to the lifestyle of a cooperative tribe and it is highly likely that private family living-units were present from a very early stage of our human evolution. There are some cases of communal dwellings but the most common form of small human settlement consisted – and in modern tribal societies still does consist – of a cluster of small huts.

The enormous advantage of this system is that it allows comparatively low-status individuals to have high status at least inside their own home units. This prevents them from becoming crushed by social competition and reduces the chances that they will seek to revenge themselves on society by means of redirected aggression. A small hut may not be a chief's hut but in terms of personal pride, even the tiniest mud cell can become a tribesman's castle.

In its earliest form these simple human settlements provided two kinds of territory – the personal and the tribal. Each hut was owned by an individual or a family unit and each village was owned by its tribe. It has been popular to think of prehistoric man as a cave-dweller but this is misleading. Where caves presented themselves as ready-made tribal homes, they were used, but they were rarities. The common form of human settlement almost certainly involved hut construction.

The oldest known example of a human hut consists today of no more than a circle of stones but they are enough to establish the astonishing fact that simple dwellings were already being built by our remote ancestors as far back as 1,900,000 years ago. The distant traces of this human urge to build were discovered recently in the Olduvai Gorge in Tanzania. They tell us that the oldest form of construction was round but they give us no idea how large the tribal group may have been. For this we have to jump forward in time.

In the French Riviera city of Nice there is a remarkable human camp site which is three hundred thousand years older than the block of flats that now covers it. When the foundations for the modern block were being excavated, it was discovered that a cluster of oval-shaped huts had been built and rebuilt there many times by our early ancestors. They had pushed branches into the sand, held them in place with rocks and curved them over to make a roof, supporting the centre of each hut with heavier vertical posts. The imprints of their post-holes were still clearly visible. While they inhabited this small settlement, these ancient hut-builders dined well on oysters, venison and wild boar. And there is evidence that, while sitting around the hearth in the middle of each of the huts, they had worked at fashioning their flint tools.

This early form of settlement was to last a very long time. If we move on from three hundred thousand years ago to a mere seven and a half thousand, we find a very similar arrangement at the neolithic settlement of Khirokitia, on a sunny hillside in southern Cyprus. Again there is a cluster of domed huts and evidence of a rich diet but new features have been added. The village has grown into a small town. Although only forty-eight round huts have been excavated so far, it is estimated that, in total, there were as many as a thousand. This meant that the human tribe had already swollen to a township of several thousand people.

The changes that had made this growth possible were the introduction of both domesticated animals and domesticated plants. Sheep and goats were now being managed and the presence of grinding stones revealed that agriculture had begun in earnest. This social control of food, producing a surplus that could be stored, meant that populations could rise dramatically.

Despite this, the small coastal town retained the age-old 'little round hut' design. The walls were stronger, the lower part being made of stone, the upper of mud brick, and both doors and windows were present. Inside, the simple space had become slightly more complex, with hearths, pits, cupboards and stoneware bowls and tables. In some cases there were upper floors with sleeping platforms. Outside, there were courtyards and, running right through the town, a paved main road.

Settlements of this type survive even today in the more remote regions of the world. Many African villages show little advance on the Stone Age settlement of Khirokitia. Where tribes have remained small and modern technology has failed to penetrate, the little round hut still thrives. But another territorial unit had already been invented, even before the domed huts of Khirokitia had been laboriously erected. This crucially important unit was 'the room'.

The curved shape of the round hut made it difficult to subdivide into cells. And it was equally difficult to join several of these primitive huts together to create a larger, more complex building. For this, a box shape was necessary. The clue came from the mud bricks used in building the earliest huts. Each brick was rectangular and they could be fitted snugly together to make a wall. This gave rise to the idea that box-shaped rooms could also be fitted snugly together. All that was necessary was to make the dwelling the same shape as the brick.

This was done as long as eight and a half thousand years ago at the Middle East site called Çatal Hüyük, in what is today modern Turkey. There, in a neolithic settlement that was occupied for nearly a thousand years, rectangular houses were grouped in tight clusters around inner courtyards. Significantly, there were back doors leading onto the communal courtyards but as yet no front doors onto the outside world. Access was via ladders. When house-owners entered, the ladder was drawn up after them and the exterior surfaces of the settlement offered nothing but a smooth, blank, defensive wall to the outside world. Only later, when building materials had become stronger, were front doors added.

Inside, there was already a division of function between the different rooms. There were eating rooms and storage rooms, living rooms and sleeping rooms. The dividing walls were originally little more than thin screens but as time passed they became heavier and thicker.

The two essential features of these dwelling designs were that they provided privacy and security. Each individual assumed a dominant role in his or her own small home-space. They could mix together on equal terms in the social areas but in the privacy of their own rooms they were in charge.

It is intriguing to contemplate the cultural impact of this architectural development of private spaces. With their new-found seclusion, our ancestors had a little more time to think. This in turn may well have led to a more rapid growth of human inventiveness and the onward march of technology. Solitary contemplation and group discussion could both take place within the boundary walls of this type of settlement. Thinking, counting, recording and planning could all blossom here, as world-shaping human activities.

This settlement system has changed little from those far off days. We still live in small rooms inside little boxes. We still subdivide the home according to several basic functions, such as eating, storage, sleeping, washing and talking. Our services, such as plumbing and lighting, have improved dramatically but essentially we still obey the age-old dwelling rules. If we have made any structural change at all, it is to provide a graded series of rooms from most public to most private.

The privacy gradient works as follows. We have maximum privacy in our bedrooms. That is where we go to rest and sleep, to dress and undress, to make love and give birth, to be sick and to die. Only our closest intimates are allowed inside the bedroom door. Next, in terms of privacy, come the bathroom and the kitchen. After that, the living room and, beyond that, the hallway. There are some people we allow into our living room but not into our bedroom. There are others that we only allow into the hallway. And there are still others who may not pass the front door.

In this way the personal or family territory is graded into a series of spaces of increasing exclusivity, making us feel more and more at ease as we get nearer to the innermost sanctuary – the bedroom. If we move in the opposite direction, out through the front door, across the garden, through the front gates and into the road, we become increasingly public. Once we are out on the streets, we become members of a new kind of social unit, for here we must share and cooperate. This is the tribal zone. Here we belong as members of a group, not as private individuals. Here we must consider ourselves occupants of a tribal territory.

This is how most people today manage to live with a deep sense of personal security. When they step inside their front gate or entrance way they feel a warm surge of familiarity. As they put their key into the lock on their front door, they experience a strong emotional reaction to the moment of 'coming home'. This simple arrangement, whether in scattered suburban houses or in high-rise apartment blocks has stayed with us for thousands of

The earliest form of human building was the round hut. As a single unit it was wonderfully efficient, but it was difficult to fit one hut onto another. Then, about eight and a half thousand years ago, someone invented the box-shaped hut and it became possible to make adjoining rooms and to build a compact settlement that could be defended against outside intruders.

years and remains almost untouched by progress – except for the novel 'furnishings and finishes' that we apply to our private rooms.

The details of the contents and decoration of the rooms in which we live are determined by three considerations: function, fashion and comfort. For example, function determines that we need a chair in which to sit down. Fashion demands that we have a chair of a particular style. The style we choose makes a statement about our personal taste and that taste in turn makes a statement about our social affiliations. Finally, comfort demands that we select a chair that will allow us to relax. The achievement of this relaxation is partly physical and partly psychological. We need soft surfaces to rest our limbs but we also need a chair that will envelop us, as if we are once again infants enjoying the embrace of our mother's arms. That is why armchairs have arms.

There are many hidden comforts in our dwellings, comforts of a psychological kind which we employ without even realizing it. The colours we choose are far from accidental. We imagine that we are decorating our rooms according to the latest fashion but there is more to it than that. There is a preferred colour in each room. This is not immediately obvious because, inevitably, there is a great deal of individual variation but if a large-scale investigation is carried out it soon emerges that we have different psychological needs in each room.

A study was made of fifteen hundred British homes. In each home seven hundred pieces of information were collected, concerning details of decoration. When the results were analysed by computer it was revealed that there is a slight but significant colour bias in each of the major rooms. We favour red in the bedroom, blue in the bathroom, orange in the kitchen, beige in the living room and green in the hallway. In psychological terms, this means that, when decorating the bedroom, we are thinking more of sex than sleep; in the bathroom, more of calm than cleanliness; in the kitchen we favour the colour of ripe fruits; in the living room we prefer the ochres of earthy security; and in the hallway we are biased towards the colours of nature. (These colours are usually diluted and muted, because we like to encourage light in our rooms, but this does not affect the bias in each case.)

Our guests respect our position when they visit us and there is little in the way of dispute for the vast majority of house-owners. Our boundary walls are honoured, even if they can be breached or scaled. They are nearly always tokens. Anyone wishing to enter a house illegally can easily do so by smashing a window. The richer households may defend themselves with special staff, television cameras, electric fences and savage dogs but the vast majority of house dwellers rely solely on mutual respect to keep them safe. Despite their vulnerability, they do not turn their homes into fortresses.

This works well enough most of the time but it also occasionally acts as a magnet to the urban outsiders – the criminal tribes nestling in the bosom of the city. These have territories of their own but for them it is not so much the personal as the gang territory that is of supreme importance. And, since it is not an officially recognized area, it must be defended more rigorously than any more orthodox patch of land.

By definition a gang territory is a defended space. To be able to defend it well, it must be made obvious to rivals. They must know when they are trespassing. This means that the territory owners must somehow advertise their presence. For a wolf or a tiger, this means leaving scent marks as they patrol their exclusive patch of land. But we are predominantly visual and so our territorial markers must be seen rather than smelt.

For ordinary home-owners, a clearly labelled front gate or front door is the classic territorial marker. But in the more hostile regions of the modern city there may be other, more dramatic visual displays. Where rival gangs roam the streets, more blatant signs are needed.

Nowhere is this more obvious than in the gangland zones of Los Angeles. Whole sectors of this vast city are dominated by warring gangs of young males. Each gang is identified in a number of ways. When they are active, the gang members wear special forms of clothing, some elements of which amount to uniforms. Their bodies are also tattooed. There is a general tattoo, consisting of a triangle of small black spots. This indicates that the person concerned is a gang member but it does not yet identify him as belonging to any one particular gang. Then, in addition, he will wear his specific gang name and emblem. Typical gang names are the Crypts and the Bloods, while some gangs are identified by the district they defend, the most powerful of all the groups going by the name of the 18th Street Gang.

When in a group together, members of the gangs also employ particular hand gestures which symbolize the names of their gangs, usually by forming the initial letters of their titles with their fingers. (It is unfortunate that one of the gangs is known locally as the

*If the city environment becomes too drab, its inhabitants rebel and add their own informal territorial decorations. In the gangland regions of Los Angeles, the walls are festooned with graffiti. Some signs are purely decorative but others display the emblems of particular gangs and act as territorial markers. Rival gang members may attempt to obliterate these signs, provoking gang warfare.*

BBC. This can cause unexpected trouble if a film crew arrives in another gang's territory and announces that it is 'from the BBC'.)

Because the gang members are not always present, they take the precaution of leaving their 'calling cards' on any permanent surface they can find. These marks are almost always made by using cans of spray paint. Although the graffiti created by the gangs frequently offend other citizens, they are an essential part of the social life of the young underworld.

There are two distinct types of wall painting: those concerned with decoration and those concerned with identification. They are made by three types of graffiti artist: the decorative painters who work on huge murals for the sheer pleasure of it; the taggers, who leave their visual 'signatures' everywhere they go; and the tag-bangers, who go around obliterating the gang signs of others and killing rival taggers.

Some taggers are 'personal' artists and may roam from territory to territory, leaving symbols that indicate 'I was here'. Others are employed by the gangs to move about, putting up the specific gang signs in as many places on the gang territory as possible. Whenever rival tag-bangers deliberately over-paint these signs there is liable to be an outbreak of gang violence.

The level of violence in the gang districts of Los Angeles is startling. All the gangs are armed with automatic weapons and, late at night, when they are high on drugs or, as the police put it, 'under the influence of controlled substances', they spray bullets at one another with remarkable zest and enthusiasm. For those who survive, the bullet holes in their bodies are proudly displayed as badges of courage. But many do not survive. Last year the authorities reported that there were 861 'gang-related homicides' in Los Angeles alone. This is more than two a night, a figure that makes the streets of Northern Ireland seem peaceful by comparison. On a bad weekend as many as twenty-five people are shot dead and it is little wonder that the authorities find ordinary policing ineffectual. All they can hope for is to contain the violence within its own social world and prevent it spreading to the rest of the city.

The income of the gangs comes from the selling of drugs or from the renting of their territories for others to sell drugs there. As long as the drugs in question remain illegal, this subculture will continue to thrive, because all attempts to eliminate the smuggling of narcotics have failed.

The existence of these unofficial, gang territories inside Los Angeles and other big cities creates a complex double culture in the urban world. Each metropolis comprises an underworld and an overworld. These two entities are usually referred to as the 'lawless' and the 'law-abiding' but this is highly inaccurate. The underworld may not obey the laws of officially accepted society but it has its own laws nonetheless. Without a set of rules, it could not function. True lawlessness means chaos, and chaos is destructive to all concerned. So we witness the development of controls and taboos within the 'lawless' world that are every bit as rigid as those in ordinary orthodox society. Anyone breaking those rules is dealt with just as severely as in the traditional courts of justice. At best the offender will lose face; at worst he will lose other parts of his anatomy. The human animal is incapable of operating without some sort of social structure. If it is not imposed by history it will be re-invented – even by those who delude themselves that they are outside all social restraints. Only the insane and the mentally retarded ignore this principle.

Territorial spacing out is not the only way in which levels of aggression can be reduced. The second major system is that of the 'peck order' or social hierarchy. This is based on personal instead of spatial relationships. If the status relationship of two people had to be resettled every time they met, considerable time and energy would be expended on aggressive actions. What the peck order system does is to establish sets of relationships that are remembered and recognized by the individuals concerned. In a gang of five males, for example, there emerges an understanding that one is the boss, a second is his number two, a third is a mid-level man, a fourth is a low-level man and the fifth is the underling. From the most dominant member of the group down to the most subordinate, there is a straight-line hierarchy, with each one knowing to whom he must look up and on whom he can look down.

In uniformed organizations, such as the police, the military or the clergy, there are specific ranks designated by specific costumes. In all other groups, although 'ranks' exist, they are usually not spelled out in any formal way. They are based, not on costume, but on the personality. When a group first forms there will be a lot of jockeying for position until natural leaders and followers have sorted themselves out. Once the members of the group have accepted their places in the peck order, they can all relax and set about their business, whatever that may happen to be. Once in a while there will be a challenge by a subordinate on his immediate superior, and a status relationship may change, but this is a rare occurrence. For the rest of the time the group can act together without undue bickering.

This system works well in small groups but in the super-tribe of the modern city it can create problems. The topmost individuals face a special dilemma. In earlier epochs they would have enjoyed a simpler challenge. As leaders they would have displayed their high status in blatant, unabashed fashion. The great prince would wear the most sumptuous clothes and the largest jewels. The warlord would display the finest suit of armour that master-craftsmen could create. If they had power, they flaunted power. Their opulence was uninhibited.

Today this has all changed. Our new leaders, while still wielding great power, must not flaunt it. Because they live in an ostensibly egalitarian society they must give the impression of being 'one of us'. How do they resolve this conflict?

The answer is that they display their power indirectly. They themselves wear dull, conventional clothing which is indistinguishable from the costume of an assistant bank manager. But they cleverly surround themselves with the trappings of power. When they walk, they are surrounded by aides and bodyguards. When they travel, they sit in specially designed limousines, flanked by motorcycle outriders. When they speak, they stand behind not one but a whole forest of microphones. In other words, the status displays have shifted from the body of the dominant figure to his support system. In this way he can convey a double message: I may be modest but I am the boss, or I may be the boss but I am modest. The message can be read either way.

To find an old-style dominant figure these days one has to search in other areas. Less sophisticated countries still occasionally throw up a peacock male, such as President Bokassa, the notorious ruler of the Central African Republic, whose rows of medals reached almost down to his feet and whose 1977 coronation, sitting on a golden throne, cost thirty million dollars in a country where the per capita annual income was a mere two hundred and fifty dollars. In show business there are a few examples but they are nearly always teetering on the brink of self-parody, as with Liberace, Elvis Presley and Michael Jackson. But these are extreme rarities.

The great stars of our time are more likely to appear unshaven and unkempt, in scruffy clothing that looks more suited to a window cleaner or a motor-cycle messenger. In taking this contrary step they are relying on a special feature of their epoch – the visual knowledge of their audience. For the great prince of yesterday, the situation was totally different. With no photography, no cinema and no television, his appearance was virtually unknown to his subjects. If he did not dress like a prince they would ignore him. But today the face of every great star is usually as familiar as that of a close family member. This means that their greatness is understood and acknowledged regardless of how they dress. By dressing like tramps they can arrogantly confront their audience with the fact that they must be accepted as dominant figures even looking like this. They are so great that they are above such matters as displaying themselves. Their mere, mumbling presence is enough for lesser mortals. This inverted form of dominance presentation is risky, however, because it is inherently insulting and sets them up as potential targets for rapid dethroning should their stardom falter.

For the lesser mortals in modern society there is a special device for enhancing status. If they lack true dominance, they can mimic it. If they cannot afford diamonds, they will wear costume jewellery. If they cannot afford Impressionist paintings, they will hang prints of Impressionists. A huge industry has grown up to produce cheap copies of priceless works of art. Honest folk-art and simple crafts have suffered as a result.

The situation is now changing. The crudity of this 'dominance mimicry' device has rendered it increasingly unsuccessful in all but the most subtle instances. It still survives in men's clothing, where high-status sporting costumes have repeatedly been raided for use as casual daywear by males who have never set foot on a sports field. This has been going on ever since the introduction of the bowler hat, the sports jacket and the sweater. (The bowler hat was originally a horseman's crash helmet, the sports jacket was a shooting coat and the sweater was borrowed from French fishermen to let everyone know that you had visited the Riviera.) Today new sports must be raided, with skiing, flying, polo, golf and athletics all providing articles of clothing to be modified as the very latest daywear.

For the ardent status seeker, none of these will do. For him, every status symbol must be the real thing. He may not be able to afford the Ferrari or the motor-yacht but he buys them anyway, borrowing money to fund his dominance displays and hoping against hope that the subterfuge will work and that he will somehow rise to the station of which he has dreamed.

In earlier days dominant figures had to flaunt their top social positions by displaying expensive, elaborate costumes. With no newspapers or television screens to make their appearance widely known, they had no choice. Today only a few dominant figures adopt this obvious form of display.

Right: Today's leaders adopt a drab costume, to persuade their followers that they are humble 'men of the people', but at the same time make it abundantly clear that they are not 'men of the people' by surrounding themselves with an elaborate and impressive entourage.

Most modern high-status individuals no longer display the trappings of power, relying instead on the dissemination of information about their personal standing through the media.

These extreme measures are the result of the super-tribal pressures. In a smaller, simpler tribe, the distance between the top and the bottom of the peck order is far less dramatic. But the contrast between the status of the city's cardboard-box street dwellers and the billionaire tycoons in their mansions is so vast that the urban status-race claims many casualties.

There are so many at the bottom and so few at the top that there are always some who will be driven to seeking revenge for what they see as their suppression and exploitation. For them, there are only two alternatives. One is to explode and destroy either others or themselves. The other is to find some kind of escape, either real or imaginary.

Strangely, real escape is rare. Few people are prepared to vacate their known environment entirely, even when it has treated them badly. They are too heavily conditioned to urban stress and a geographical escape to a remote bolt-hole has little appeal. Instead they seek various illusions of escape, while staying firmly put in their familiar surroundings.

*The more drab and repetitive the daily routine, the more people need moments of great celebration as a compensation. The world's greatest carnivals and festivals take place in cities where they provide a dramatic contrast with the other days of the year.*

These illusory escapes are of several kinds. Always popular and always forbidden has been the device of 'chemical dreaming'. The taking of drugs as relief from the tedium or the intense pressure of city life has been commonplace for thousands of years. Unfortunately, the most powerful drugs have always been a severe health hazard and for that reason have never been accepted. Despite this, for many communities they have become the popular crutch that props people up through the depressing day and the hideous night.

For others, there has always been the more harmless alternative of 'fantasy dreaming'. Through novels, films and television programmes, they live out exciting lives by proxy. If they themselves cannot travel around the world in eighty days, they can at least watch somebody else doing so and identify with him as best they can.

Others look for more active, creative outlets to relieve their boredom and their feelings of oppression. They may take part in some kind of adult play – becoming fanatical about certain kinds of sports, hobbies or games. Or they may focus their attention on annual celebrations – carnivals, festivals and other forms of ceremonial excitement. Or they may opt for deliberate risk taking, by gambling or taking part in dangerous pursuits. Finally,

The designs of cities have
become increasingly
impersonal and less suited to
the character of the human
animal. Occasionally there is a
minor rebellion against this
trend, with the erection of
strange and idiosyncratic
buildings that defy
regimentation. Two examples
of this are the Hundertwasser
house in Vienna and the Gaudi
church in Barcelona (above).

they may turn to special novelties, in the form of bizarre cults, strange fads or outlandish types of vice. In all these ways they seek to obliterate the pain of growing up in the nagging tension of the urban cauldron – the human zoo.

Despite the obvious disadvantages of living in conditions so unnatural for the tribal human species, the fact remains that millions of people do stay put in the cities, and these centres do grow bigger and bigger each year. Los Angeles, for example, is already so vast that it is now half the size of Belgium. So urban life must have some powerful appeal for the human animal and it is not difficult to see what that is. The very qualities that cause the citizen so much pain also provide a special reward. Just because it destroys the peaceful tribal existence of a small village, modern urban life frees the individual from the constraints of tradition and permits innovation on a grand scale. Novelty, which would seem out of place in a small village, feels strangely right in the stimulating atmosphere of the big town. Here, invention, science and the arts can all flourish.

The problem for the future is to find ways of keeping this valuable part of city life while losing its hazards. The secret is to make the city centre so stimulating and entertaining that it provokes a creative rather than a destructive response. Architecture that is playfully idiosyncratic excites people, just as architecture which is boringly businesslike, repetitive and predictable dulls their minds. Commerce, the ideal servant of the city, has too often become its master. It is possible to move down many modern city streets and feel the drab greyness spreading from the bleak, flat walls. Wild, extravagantly imaginative ideas are possible in city design but they hardly ever see bricks and mortar. Wilfully unusual and provocative architecture is an extreme rarity.

It is not that we are incapable of producing a stimulating urban scene. When great exhibitions or special leisure centres are designed, imaginative architecture is given full rein. But for some reason it is hardly ever felt necessary to introduce this element of fun into the ordinary city landscape. When, by some rare chance, an artist is permitted to create an imaginative building in the middle of a city, as with the Hundertwasser House in Vienna or the Gaudi buildings in Barcelona, people flock to see them and relish their oddity. Despite their reactions, nobody in authority seems to respond to the impact such projects are able to make.

When graffiti gangs spend hours decorating the grimy walls of their dingy ghettos with

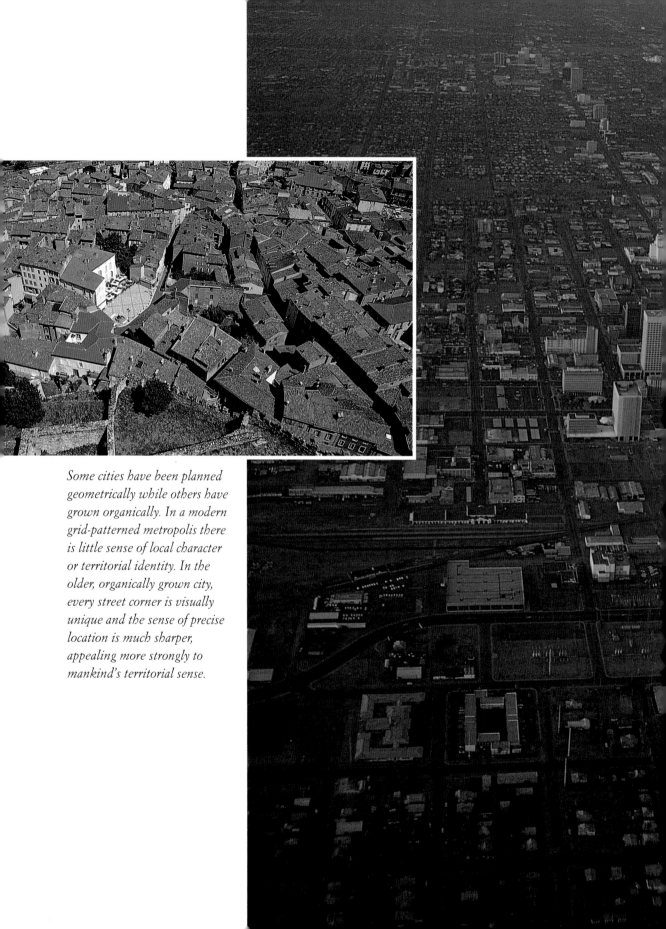

Some cities have been planned geometrically while others have grown organically. In a modern grid-patterned metropolis there is little sense of local character or territorial identity. In the older, organically grown city, every street corner is visually unique and the sense of precise location is much sharper, appealing more strongly to mankind's territorial sense.

The growth of a city does not
necessarily mean that it must
lose its human dimension. Even
in the vast urban concentration
that is modern-day Cairo, local
identity is not lost. In theory it
is possible for the urbanite to
have the best of both worlds –
the stimulating excitement of
the city centre, and the cosy,
ancient feeling of belonging to
a small local tribal group.

bright signs and symbols, until they resemble vast works of abstract art, nobody gets the message: that man needs to adorn his world with playful inventiveness. The typical reaction is to label the graffiti artists as vandals and to pray for the dull greyness to return.

These are not trivial matters. It is clear that the kind of environment in which we live has a massive impact on our behaviour. If we design our cities like old-fashioned zoos, we must expect to see our citizens pacing miserably up and down their human zoo cages. If we design our cities like exotic game parks, then we can expect to see our citizens respond in an entirely different way.

There is no reason why the human animal cannot live successfully in great city complexes. If we remember that evolution has not had time to change the tribal hunting species to which we all belong, we should be able to enjoy the urban stimulation while avoiding the urban strain. If we adapt the city to the basic nature of the human animal, instead of trying to force the human animal to adapt to the city, anything should be possible.

This means providing a more satisfying tribal existence without removing the special excitements of the big city. It means living in real, local communities, each with its own unique flavour, all of which have access to the large-scale stimulation centres. It means redesigning our cities almost from scratch. They have grown haphazardly and are now like elephants trying to fly. Somehow we must change these elephants into jumbo jets. This must be the challenge of the twenty-first century if we are to avoid the fate of so many great civilizations that have gone before us.

It is a sobering experience to encounter one of today's mega-cities. A visit to Cairo, for example, can give a glimpse of how things can go wrong and how they can be made to go right. Cairo at present boasts a throbbing mass of fifteen million citizens. By the year 2000 this will have risen to nearly twenty million, because each day another thousand new citizens are added to the total. Already the traffic jams linger on until the early hours of the morning. The future looks bleak, yet within the seething mass of humanity it is still possible to find local communities with special identities. Much of the architecture has managed to remain at the human level. Only where newly designed, tall, soulless blocks of apartments have been added are the local inhabitants beginning to show signs of despair.

Despite its increasingly suffocating chaos, Cairo has somehow been able to retain the village atmosphere in many of its older districts. They may be rammed tightly together but each locality contrives to keep alive the tribal sense of belonging to a small patch of human social activity. Ultimately, even this may be swamped out and then we may well see the return of nothing short of a Biblical pestilence.

This may sound melodramatic but consider the facts. Any species that overcrowds itself beyond a certain point shows seven stages of damage: 1 Individuals become psychologically stressed. 2 This stress causes physiological disturbances. 3 These disturbances weaken the body's natural defence mechanisms. 4 This weakening makes people increasingly vulnerable to infection. 5 The overcrowding makes it possible for infections to spread like wildfire. 6 The infections grow until they become epidemics. 7 The epidemics decimate the populations.

This is what happens to lemmings when there is a 'lemming year'. If these small rodents overbreed in a particular season, they soon start to suffer from stress diseases and rush madly in all directions. They do not commit suicide, as popular myth would have it, but instead exhaust their body defence mechanisms until, finally, most of them die from stress-related diseases.

Although we have not yet reached the lemming condition, we are already showing signs of edging in that direction. We get a hint of this whenever there is a flu epidemic. Those who are already unfit, or weakened in some way by their modern lifestyles, are the ones who are most likely to succumb to the advancing waves of flu virus. Already, flu epidemics have killed more people than the whole of human warfare.

Most people who catch flu do still survive, however. But what if a more virulent, lethal disease were to mutate and become as easy to catch as the common cold? Then we would see our great cities crumble and collapse. Of all the doomsday scenarios, this is the most likely. Our best method of protection is to ensure that our natural defence mechanisms are not in a weakened condition. This means reducing urban stress as much as possible.

It has been calculated that by the year 2000 half the world's human population will be housed in cities and that there will be at least twenty-six mega-cities, each with over ten million inhabitants. Most of these cities will be found in the Third World. Whether they turn out to be breeding grounds for human inventiveness and creativity or for lethal diseases and epidemics remains to be seen. Gigantic playgrounds or vast ghost towns – the choice is up to us.

# 4

# *The Biology of Love*

When I described human beings as the sexiest primates alive, some people thought I was being merely titillating but that was not the case. I was making an accurate scientific statement.

During the course of evolution, something very strange happened to our patterns of sexual behaviour. We extended our sexuality in several new ways. I am not referring here to our cultural variations and excesses, where certain societies have become obsessed with particular kinds of erotic expression. I am talking about basic changes in our sexual biology which apply to all humans, everywhere, at all times.

Many other animals, for example, restrict their sexual activities to one short period of the year. During this breeding season they are intensely active but at all other times they become completely non-sexual. Their level of sex hormones drops, they stop producing eggs and sperm, and they also often lose their special display organs and bright colours, becoming camouflaged and dowdy in appearance.

Human beings have abandoned a limited breeding season and are prepared to mate at any time of year. Eggs and sperm are shed all year round and there is never a non-breeding season. Nor do we change physically in appearance from one season to the next. It may be true that, in the spring, a young man's fancy is specially aroused but that does not mean that he spent the previous winter in some kind of sexual hibernation. Nor that, in the autumn, he will enter a monastery.

Other primates do not indulge in a prolonged courtship sequence. We do. There are many stages between the initial meeting of male and female and the final moment of sexual consummation. It is true that certain societies have attempted to suppress this natural human tendency, either for puritanical or economic reasons, but wherever young adults are given sufficient freedom of expression, they display the typically elaborate courting behaviour of our species. Indeed, even in those societies where such activities are heavily penalized, they keep on resurfacing, frequently at considerably risk to the individuals involved. Even where this behaviour is punishable by death, lovers will manage to meet secretly and whisper sweet nothings to one another, as the powerful sexual longings of the human animal force their way to the surface.

Once the couple have completed their courtship and mating has begun, there is another demonstration of the way we have extended our sexuality. Instead of the brief, impersonal, eight-second mating act of the typical baboon, the human couple indulge in prolonged pre-copulatory actions. At the climax of these lengthy erotic interludes, the act of copulation itself is also much longer. Yes, we are capable of quick, ape-like matings but given good health and sufficient privacy, we are likely to spend at least a hundred times longer at our sexual encounters than most other monkeys and apes.

The biggest change in sexual behaviour has occurred in the human female. She has extended her sexuality in four ways. First, she has evolved an intense orgasmic climax to copulation. This is unique among primates. The females of some other species have been observed to experience a mini-orgasm but nothing that even approaches the earth-moving response of the climactic human female.

Second, she has extended her period of sexual receptivity throughout her monthly menstrual cycle. Most other primate females limit their sexual activities to a brief period around the time of their monthly ovulation. At other moments in the cycle they are both unattracted to the males and unattractive to them. By contrast, the human female is ready to mate at any time, regardless of whether she is capable of being fertilized. This means that about three-quarters of her natural sexual activity has nothing to do with procreation.

Third, she has concealed the timing of her ovulation. Not only is she prepared to mate at other times but she has even gone to the length of hiding the moment when she can conceive. Other primates usually show conspicuous sexual swellings in the genital region when ovulating and, even in those species that do not show these swellings, there is a marked change in female behaviour or in female odour. There are no detectable changes of this kind in the human female. This means that, to be sure of fertilizing her egg, the human male must mate time after time after time – another major increase in sexual activity for our species.

Fourth, she is even prepared to mate when she is pregnant. And finally, she will also continue to do so after the menopause and into old age, long after her breeding ability has come to an end.

No other primate behaves like this. We make love more often, more intensely and for longer than any other monkey or ape. The only species that begins even to approach our sexual appetite is our closest living relative, the bonobo or pygmy chimpanzee.

So I was entirely justified in my controversial remark that we are the sexiest of all the primates. This is not some sort of cultural decadence but a major trend in our evolutionary progress. It gives us some of our most sublime moments and also, inevitably, some of our greatest agonies.

Sexual prudery and puritanism are the codes of conduct that are inappropriate for our species, not sensuality and eroticism. But why has this happened? What has changed us so dramatically?

Before trying to answer that question, it will help to take a closer look at the human sexual sequence, from the moment that boy meets girl to the point where they are enjoying full sexual contact. How does adult intimacy begin? How do young males and females take the first crucial steps that will eventually lead to total intimacy?

In each culture there is the initial problem of how boy does manage to meet girl. Where adults have borrowed sexual activity for use in economic or other non-sexual spheres, the first meetings may be highly artificial. Arranged marriages completely stifle and eliminate the early phases of the courtship sequence. The young couple are brought together formally, exposed to a bonding ritual of some kind and then left to sort our their personal sexuality in the privacy of a marriage bed.

If this rigid interference is avoided, then young people will find some way to meet and mingle informally, and to select suitable partners. This may happen almost accidentally as part of ordinary social life, or special 'arena displays' may take place. In these, unattached males and females gather in certain favoured spots, or 'display grounds', where they can scrutinize one another. This is frequently done under the guise of performing some other activity, such as drinking, eating or dancing.

Parties, dances and other social gatherings are specially organized to help overcome the initial awkwardness. At all of these, there is the mild pretence that something other than courtship is taking place. This rather transparent subterfuge means that, if no amorous contact is initiated, individual failures are not obvious.

More direct examples ignore this. At the dating agencies and in the singles bars of the

Western world, there is no attempt to conceal the true reason for the coming together. If failure occurs, it cannot be overlooked and there exists, inevitably, an air of slight desperation at such places.

Less deliberately organized gatherings manage to avoid this problem. Around the shores of the Mediterranean there is an attractive tradition that sees young people parading up and down the main streets of the towns and along the seafronts in the early evening. These parades, encouraged by the climate, are a casual daily event during which the males and females are able to eye one another and start to make the first tentative contacts. For the youngest of the teenagers, this is the start of a lengthy process of mate selection. There will be many false starts and fumbling mistakes. Inexperience, uncertainty and lack of self-confidence hold the young adults back but their growing sense of sexual excitement drives them on.

One of the biggest problems for young couples in these arena displays is how to break away from their childhood groups. Boys have played with boys, girls with girls. Now, when a new bond between boy and girl is forged, it is as though they are both being disloyal to their earlier companions. And the matter is made more difficult because the members of these same-sex groups often oppose the new contacts, knowing that they spell the end of a phase. The childhood gang is about to collapse and it resists the process as best it can.

As the new couples begin to form, the hesitant partners go through an ambivalent stage during which they enjoy increasingly intimate moments with one another but repeatedly return to their old unisex 'tribes' to report back on what has happened. Despite the carefully manoeuvred privacy of their new, heterosexual moments, they cannot resist sharing their novel experiences with their earlier 'gang'. Then, as the pair bond begins to grow stronger and the gang bond begins to weaken, there comes the moment when they refuse to divulge a shared intimacy. The exclusivity of their lovers' relationship has begun.

From this point on, the couple spend more and more private time together. This is the information-exchange phase, when they discover just how much they have in common. There must already be considerable sexual interest in one another to have reached this stage. Sexual appeal is no longer the issue. What is taking place is more than a sexual act, it is a full pair-formation. If they pursue the relationship further, they must be sure that they can not only copulate well together but also spend days and nights, weeks and months,

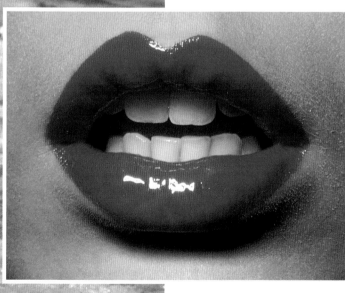

*Young adults display powerful
gender signals to one another.
The male develops broader
shoulders, a more muscular
body and a deeper voice. The
female develops wider hips with
rounded buttocks. The paired
hemispheres of her buttocks are
echoed in her rounded breasts.
Her enlarged, reddened lips
echo her genitals.*

years and even decades together, as they rear their offspring. This is not a step to be taken lightly, with the result that most human courtships take a considerable amount of time.

How does the sequence begin? What are the signals that a member of the opposite sex transmits to arouse interest? For many mammals, the very first trigger is a special smell. When two dogs meet, almost their first act is to sniff one another. From the odours their noses encounter, the dogs can tell one another's precise sexual condition.

For humans, sexual body fragrance is also important but that comes later. In the early stages the main impact comes from visual signals. Here we have a special problem because of our unique vertical posture. The visual signals of other female primates are transmitted largely from the rear. When the female is on heat she develops sexual swellings on her rump which are visible from a distance, or she gives off a special sexual fragrance. These powerful signals act as a magnet to the males, which approach her to examine them more closely. If the males become aroused, they will mount and mate with the female from behind, while she stands on all fours. This must also have been the method used by our primeval ancestors before we reared up onto our hind legs and evolved into the bipedal condition.

At that point, when we stood up, two things happened. First, we had to develop a new kind of rear end. We needed better-developed muscles on our rumps to keep us upright. These new muscles bulged on our behinds and gave us something unique among all monkeys and apes: rounded buttocks. The two new hemispheres of flesh became our primary female sexual signal. Unfortunately, however, when a male and a female human walked towards one another, the buttocks were no longer visible. The new walking posture that had given us our special rump signal had now hidden it from view. Something had to be done to make the frontal display of the female more exciting.

The answer was to provide her with imitation buttocks on the front of her body. Like other female primates she was already prone to develop swellings on her chest when giving milk to her infants but these would disappear again when she stopped lactating. The evolutionary trick was to stop these swellings from deflating. If they could be kept there permanently and increased in size until they too became paired, fleshy hemispheres, then the human female could signal her sexuality from in front as well as from behind.

The female breasts evolved, quite simply, as buttock mimics. Support for this idea is found in the anatomy of the breasts. The bulk of their shape (about two-thirds of it) is formed by fatty tissue that plays no part in milk production. The glandular part that is concerned with feeding the infant constitutes only a small proportion (about one-third). In other words, the rounded female human breasts are more concerned with sexual display than with maternal feeding. In fact flat-chested women are often better at feeding their infants than heavy-breasted women. The heavy breast tends to suffocate the baby as it struggles to suck the nipple.

The breasts reach their maximum roundedness in the late teens, the optimum time for sexual signalling. After that they begin to sag slightly but remain swollen for many years until, in old age, they finally droop and lose their rounded shape. As a gender signal, therefore, they transmit their message throughout the entire female reproductive phase, from menarche (first menstruation) to menopause.

So the basic female sexual signal of our species consists of paired, fleshy hemispheres. In addition to the buttocks and breasts, the general roundedness of the adult female body helps to echo this pattern and reinforce it. Her curved shoulders and her smooth knees can also act, in a minor way, as paired hemisphere signals. Many female postures during the courtship phase help to display these four locations – buttocks, breasts, shoulders and knees – to the watching male.

In the Western world clothing can be used to help display these features. Sexual 'daring' has involved many variations of the 'rounded flesh exposure' theme, from off-the-shoulder styles that expose the curvature of the shoulders, to low-cut dresses that reveal the upper curve of the breasts, to short skirts that bring the smooth knees into prominence. The buttocks themselves – the primary signal of which the others are all echoes – are too strong a display and remain covered in ordinary social situations, emerging from hiding only on the beach.

The extent of these displays varies according to the mood of the female. A recent research project that measured the amount of bare flesh displayed by females dancing in night-clubs made a remarkable discovery. It emerged that the females unconsciously increased the amount of flesh exposed by their costumes at precisely the times when they were ovulating. They were not aware of this – it was only discovered later, when information about their sexual cycles was assembled and analysed. They themselves had not calculated that they were ovulating and had no idea that they were varying their displays according to their physiological condition. This shows just how basic and unconscious human sexual behaviour can be.

Similar display differences can be observed, not merely in individuals, but in whole cultures. In the Western world, during the present century, the amount of bare leg displayed by female skirts has varied from decade to decade. It was, for example, large in the 1920s and the 1960s, which were boom periods, and small in the 1930s and 1970s, which were depressed periods. The buoyant mood of the affluent periods encourages the female to display her legs boldly; the sad mood of the depressed periods makes her cover herself up. Again, she is not aware at the time that she is making these changes, merely that they are 'fashionable'. But it is human sexuality that drives these changes, not the heads of fashion houses.

Turning to the female genitals themselves, these are also largely concealed by the standing position. In monkeys and apes the genital region is clearly visible from behind and can act as an obvious sexual signal. This is not the case for human females. Again, they need an echo – some form of body self-mimicry – to transmit a genital signal that can more easily be seen by the approaching male. The answer lies in the female lips.

Unlike the tight lips on the faces of other primates, the human female (and to a lesser extent, the human male) has lips that have been turned inside out. When we look at the lips of the human female, what we are, in effect, seeing is part of the inside of her mouth, everted and highly visible. The shape and colour of these everted lips have evolved as a mimic of the genital labia that are now hidden from view between the female's vertical legs.

As if to emphasize this mimicry, these newly evolved, uniquely human lips become engorged with blood during sexual arousal, making them larger and redder, a change that is also simultaneously occurring with the hidden labia. To increase the effect even more, many females, from ancient Egypt to the modern day, have painted their lips even redder.

In recent years cosmetic surgeons in Europe and the United States have introduced special techniques for artificially enlarging the female lips into a permanent, sexy pout. Implants of collagen or silicone are used by some, while others favour surgery that turns the lips even further out into a mega-pout. Creating what is known as the 'Paris pout' or 'bee-sting lips', these procedures have secretly been applied to the faces of many well-known actresses and models, whose natural lips offered only an average pout, when their professional roles required them to be super-normal.

In addition to this genital self-mimicry, the human female also displays her adult, reproductive condition by her general body shape. At puberty the angular schoolgirl suddenly becomes much more curvaceous. As her breasts swell, her hips widen, giving her a conspicuous waist. This new, sexual silhouette contrasts with the shape of the pubertal male, whose body becomes increasingly top-heavy, with wider shoulders, a broader chest and more powerful arm muscles. Underlying this gender contrast is a huge difference in adult body tissues. The human female body has almost twice as much fat in its constitution as the male. The average female body contains twenty-eight per cent fat, the average male only fifteen per cent.

Both sexes display their newly acquired adult condition by growing tufts of hair in the region of the armpits and genitals. At a distance, these can act as visual displays of sexual maturity but they are more concerned with scent signalling during the later stages of courtship. There are numerous skin glands producing sexual scents around the armpits and genitals, and the hair tufts trap the fragrance of these scents. On clean bodies these are powerfully erotic but beneath layers of clothing they can quickly deteriorate and become stale. Because of this, anti-perspirants and deodorants are frequently used today, on the principle that having no smell at all is better than a good smell gone bad.

Males also signal their adult masculinity by their deeper voices and their hairy faces. Even when removed by shaving, the male beard is still clearly visible as a slightly roughened, darkened area of facial skin. As a bony support for the male beard, the masculine jaw is heavier. It juts out more and is longer.

There are many other minor, visible gender differences between the young male and the young female. Male bodies are generally more muscular, with bigger hands and feet, and usually a light scattering of body hairs. Female bodies are softer and smoother to the touch.

This skin smoothness is a powerful erotic signal for our species. When a survey of sex appeal was carried out in two hundred different cultures, it was discovered that clean skin was the single most important feature. Dirtiness, poor complexion, pimples and other skin disorders were all universally disliked in a sexual context. (It is a sad irony that excessive acne is always found sexually unappealing, when it is a condition that happens to be associated with a particularly high level of sex hormones and an intense sex drive.)

These skin reactions are undoubtedly linked to a primeval avoidance of disease. In evolutionary terms it would pay a young adult, seeking a mate, to keep away from any member of the opposite sex who might be carrying a serious disease. This inborn response would not be sensitive enough to distinguish between serious and trivial skin conditions. It would take no chances, leaving our species with a strong preference for clean and unblemished partners. (The whole of the modern cosmetics industry is based on this ancient biological preference.)

Returning to the differences between the sexes, even where there are no biological

*Throughout history young males and females have sought ways of exaggerating their gender signals. Males have worn wide epaulettes to increase their shoulder width and females have worn bustles and crinolines to emphasize their buttocks and hips.*

gender contrasts, we invent them culturally. Our clothing, our body adornments and our special, local, skin decorations all help to emphasize the visual divergence between the two sexes. This applies in particular to head-hair which, surprisingly, shows no biological differences at puberty. If untouched, the hair of both the young male and young female human will grow extraordinarily long. No other monkey or ape displays this strange feature and it was almost certainly one of the original 'flags' of our species, identifying our primeval ancestors as a new type of animal. Bodily, we may have become the naked ape but on top of our heads we became the excessively long-haired ape.

If left uncut, our adult head-hair would reach down to our waists. Each head-hair grows for six years, to a length of some forty inches or a hundred centimetres, before falling out. But few human cultures can bear to leave such flowing tresses untouched. Almost

everywhere, they are modified and converted into yet another gender signal.

So, with all our biological sex signals and our cultural embellishments on display, we stand before one another. We eye one another from a distance and contemplate our first move. The sequence is nearly always the same, give or take a few details.

First, we look. We analyse the visual appeal of young adults of the opposite sex. Once we have made our choice, we contrive ways of engaging in eye-to-eye contact. Staring at strangers is nearly always threatening behaviour, so we have to break down that barrier. With a soft smile and a slightly longer than average gaze, we signal our sexual interest.

If the soft smile is returned, we take the next step – making vocal contact. We exchange a few meaningless comments. We busy ourselves with trivial, irrelevant activities which we can share.

*Although human courtship sequences vary enormously around the globe they tend to follow the same general pattern, from the first visual encounter to the final genital contact. Six typical stages are shown here:*

- *Mutual gaze – no body contact.*
- *Simple body contact – arm on shoulder.*
- *Frontal body contact – the embrace.*
- *Mouth contact – the kiss.*
- *Intimate contact – hand explores body.*
- *Mouth explores body.*

At the same time we are checking the companion's voice, accent, dialect, tonality, liveliness, cheerfulness and curiosity. This stage is easy to break off. If the small-talk does not reveal a compatible partner, we can quickly dissolve the new relationship without hurting feelings.

One way in which we can find out how our new companion is reacting towards us is to prolong our periods of close-proximity gazing. During these early stages of courtship the eyes transmit vital signals. If we stare closely enough we can detect the degree of pupil dilation as they look back at us. Since the pupils expand slightly more than usual when they see something they like, we can tell whether we are 'being liked' or not. If our companion's eyes show huge, black pupils, we know that they find us appealing and that the next stage in our courtship sequence will probably meet with success. If, on the other hand, the pupils shrink to pin-pricks when we gaze closely at our companion's face, we might as well give up.

The pupils cannot lie because we have no conscious control over them. And normally, of course, our response to them is also unconscious. We get a 'feeling' that we are liked or disliked, without understanding quite how we know this. No wonder young lovers spend so much time together, head to head, staring into one another's eyes as they whisper and chat.

The next stage takes us over an important threshold. For this involves physical contact. Initially this is often disguised as an accidental contact or some kind of helpful adjustment. Taking hold of a hand to help someone over an obstacle is a classic 'first touch' strategy, for example. An introductory handshake that lingers a little longer than usual is an alternative. Eventually, when the pair have agreed to share an event together, the hand-in-hand contact is the earliest and most innocent of all the possible body contacts that could be made.

Closer contact can be introduced by the arm round the shoulder. This brings the two bodies closer together and enables them to touch flanks in a modest way. The arm around the waist is a further step in this direction, bringing even greater intimacy.

The full embrace comes next, accompanied in most cultures by mouth-to-mouth kissing. This stage in the sequence may be postponed in some societies, where public kissing is taboo. Even there, however, it will surface in the more private moments of the couple.

Hand to head is the next phase. This may sound an innocuous contact but it is not. It has about it a special sense of intimacy, because the head is a strongly guarded region of the body. It contains a concentration of vital sense organs and these have to be protected as carefully as possible. So there must be great trust before the new partner is allowed full freedom to caress the facial region.

Next, the hands of the companion are permitted to stray over the body. These hand-to-body contacts are the first sign that serious sexual interest is beginning to build. The previous stages can all be disguised in some way, as if they are really social actions without any sexual significance, but when hands start to caress the more intimate regions of the partner's body, all pretence has to cease. Now, if one member of the pair wishes to stop the partner's progress, there is nothing for it but to have a row. Any male who has moved to this phase too quickly – like the office groper or the party mauler – will find himself in trouble, risking everything from a demeaning rejection to a charge of sexual harassment.

Beyond this stage there lies the full sexual intimacy of young lovers, involving advances that include hand to breast, mouth to breast, hand to genitals and, finally, genitals to genitals. These stages usually only occur when the couple, after a long courtship phase, have at last decided to form a pair. They lead, inevitably, to copulation.

Clearly, the general sequence outlined here is a simplification but if a large number of specific sequences were recorded and analysed, with the results pooled and then averaged, the final picture would look much as I have described it. When we are falling in love we may feel unique but the truth is that we are all highly predictable, down to the smallest gesture and glance. In fact, film of young couples shot in wildly differing cultures all around the world shows remarkable similarities during this particular phase of the human life-cycle. The shy smiles and sidelong glances of the young female, the forward tilt of the body of the young male as he questions her and playfully shows off, these and a hundred other fleeting moments of human courtship are universals. They are understood across language barriers and class distinctions, and follow an almost identical pattern in the human pair-formation ritual.

The advantage of this gradual sequence is that it allows either partner to drop out of the pairing process before matters have gone too far. At each stage the couple are learning more and more about each other and are increasingly aware of how well suited (or unsuited) they may be for one another. In this respect it is very similar to the pair-formation rituals of other species.

In the later stages of intimacy, when courtship has progressed to the pre-copulatory stage, additional factors come into play. Mutual discovery may still be in operation but now sexual arousal is also important. As the couple embrace and explore one another's bodies, they are also unconsciously checking one another's levels of physiological excitement. Four things are now happening at once: they are learning still more about one another as individuals; they are arousing themselves sexually; they are arousing their partners sexually; and they are synchronizing their arousals.

The synchronization of sexual arousal is especially important in our species. This is because, when male and female orgasms coincide, there is a powerful, shared emotional experience that tightens the bond of attachment between them. Also, if the orgasms are timed to occur close to one another, this gives the highest chance of successful fertilization.

This double orgasm is not always easy to achieve, usually because the male reaches climax before the female is ready. This is common in young males but it is not too serious a problem because these same males are nearly always capable of ejaculating several times in fairly quick succession, giving time for the female to catch up. Older males usually cannot do this but they compensate for their lower virility by taking much longer to reach climax in the first place. Either way, the female is likely to be strongly aroused before the sexual encounter is fully completed.

What form does this arousal take? How does the body of the male and female human change during the sexual sequence? In both sexes there is vaso-congestion. The best way to understand this is to think of the human blood system as a network of highways. When vaso-congestion occurs, there is a traffic jam. Blood flows into certain vessels more quickly than it flows out. The vessels concerned are those on or near the surface of the body, with the result that the skin becomes flushed and the softer parts of the visible anatomy become enlarged and engorged with blood.

The sensations created by these changes are strongly erotic. There is a feeling of heat and heightened sensitivity all over the body surface. On the chest a bright sex flush may appear. Nipples become erect. The nose becomes swollen. Ear-lobes also swell and become sensitive to oral caresses.

In the female, the lips – of both the mouth and the genitals – become redder and more swollen. They are increasingly responsive to the slightest touch. The breasts enlarge by up to twenty-five per cent. In the male, the lips also become more sensitive and the penis becomes swollen with blood, until the pressure is so great that it is hard and fully erect.

The human penis is a strange structure. In other primates there is an 'os penis' – a small penis-bone with which the males can achieve a quick and easy erection. As soon as they have started to become aroused, their penis-bone flips the penis up into an erect condition. In the human male the penis-bone has vanished. Somewhere in our evolutionary past we abandoned this efficient aid to quick sexual readiness. This unique human feature appears to be part of the slowing down process of the copulation sequence. The male has to become strongly aroused before his penis will become sufficiently erect to allow insertion in the vagina. If he is abnormally stressed or unhealthy, he will find it much harder to gain an erection than if he had the aid of a penis-bone, which could click into action at the slightest tremor of sexuality. This evolutionary 'handicap' has the effect of ensuring that human males who copulate successfully are also physically vigorous and healthy, and therefore suitable candidates for future parenthood. In this way, the boneless human penis is closely linked to the evolution of the pair bond and paternal care.

When fully erect, the human penis is also much larger than that of other apes, not only in length but also in width. (The erect penis of the gorilla is only two inches/five centimetres long and that of the chimpanzee is a thin spike.) This increase in size is clearly associated with the prolonged human copulation sequence and the stimulation of the female to a full and intense orgasm, something that is denied to other primate females. (Both chimpanzees and gorillas take only fifteen seconds to copulate.)

A curious myth perpetuated by modern 'sex manuals' is that human penis size is unimportant. This appears to be a sop to protect the egos of those males most likely to need to read such books. If it were true, the evolution in human males of the largest penis of all the primates – larger even than that of the mighty gorilla – would be hard to explain. The simple fact is that a larger penis is physically more stimulating to the human female, although it goes without saying that a much-loved male with a small penis will be more arousing than a little-loved male with a large one. However, given equal emotional attachment, the bigger penis will always win.

The human female equivalent of the male penis – the clitoris, a tiny lump of flesh lying just above the genital opening – also becomes erect during sexual arousal. It is lavishly supplied with nerve endings and its repeated massage during pelvic thrusting adds considerably to the heightening of female arousal.

Heavily armed with this elaborate sexual equipment, the human couple proceed to lick, suck, probe, clasp, stroke, squeeze and caress themselves into a state of abandoned sexual excitement. In place of the cursory mounting, ejaculation and dismounting of most other primates, the human lovers twine, writhe and moan with prolonged pleasure. The fact that it is shared pleasure of an intense kind makes it a crucial aid to pair-bonding. In this way, as well as helping to ensure fertilization, it increases the chances of the successful rearing of any subsequent offspring, where the addition of paternal care to the obligatory maternal care plays an important role in child survival.

At the beginning of the final, copulatory stage of the sexual sequence, a crucial threshold is passed with the insertion of the penis, now three inches/eight centimetres longer than in its resting condition, into the vagina. At the same time the aroused vagina lengthens and becomes distended. Sexual excitement also produces greatly increased secretions which lubricate the genitals and make the pelvic thrusts of the male smoother and more efficient.

While this is happening, there is a great increase in blood pressure and pulse and breathing rates. The heart beats at twice its normal speed as orgasm approaches. Blood pressure also doubles, the body sweats profusely and breathing becomes increasingly noisy and difficult, as though the mating couple are running a race.

At the moment of female orgasm there are rhythmic contractions of the vagina at intervals of 0.8 of a second. When the male ejaculates, the contractions of the penis that expel the sperm occur at precisely the same rate. This means that a simultaneous orgasmic experience can be synchronized to an astonishing degree, creating an intense, psychological feeling of 'oneness'.

This, then, is the sexual pattern of our species. When we describe it as 'making love', we are being precise. That is exactly what it is. The lavishness of our erotic behaviour serves us well as loving partners in what is to follow – the longest parental sequence known in the entire animal kingdom.

If the pair-bond is so important to the human species, then an obvious question springs to mind: why does it break down so often? Why are there so many sexual triangles, adulteries, annulments, separations and divorces? Why are human adults not all programmed for permanent, faithful coupling? If the need is so powerful, why is the bond so weak?

Since the pair-bond's primary function is to defend the offspring by doubling the parental care they receive, then, as far as the children are concerned, it should be perfect and total. In an ideal world their parents should remain faithful and love one another for ever. This will protect the next generation, first as helpless babies, then as vulnerable infants, as growing children, as parents themselves (by providing helpful grandparents) and as ageing adults (as inheritors of their parents' estate). Any breakdown in this pair-bond distresses and threatens them.

Why is this threat ignored? Several answers have been given to this burning question – on a subject that has spawned thousands of films and countless novels. The first answer sees the pair-bond as a new evolutionary trend that has yet to be perfected. Other monkeys and apes, it is argued, rarely form pairs. Our species has moved away from their sexual norm so recently that our pair-bonding mechanism is still evolving. One day it will be fully expressed but at the moment all we can observe is an incomplete prototype.

It is hard to accept this explanation. There is no evidence that pair-bonds of any animal species are particularly powerful. It is not that we have a weak bond compared with other pairing animals. Ours is as good as most and is probably fully developed. Careful studies of pairing birds have revealed that in every nest there will probably be at least one egg that was not fathered by the 'husband' of the female in question.

Konrad Lorenz, the great Austrian naturalist whose studies of the social lives of geese have become world-famous, was once surprised to find that one of his favourite geese had been unfaithful to its long-standing mate. He asked an assistant to go and check the records of all his geese. She returned to inform him that unfaithfulness was widespread in his flocks of birds. He looked so startled by this news that she blurted out: 'Don't worry, professor, after all, geese are only human'.

If pair-bonds are never perfect, what is it that holds them back? What advantage could their imperfection have, for both us and other animals? One answer lies in the need to

avoid wasting a good, healthy, reproductive adult when its mate has been killed. When a long-term partner is suddenly lost, there is a period of acute distress. In humans this period of mourning lasts from a few months to many years. For a few individuals it lasts a lifetime and their reproductive potential is never realized. The same is true of other species. In most, the distress lasts for some days, even weeks. Eventually they will set up a new pair-bond with a fresh partner but once in a while they will mourn for much longer.

It follows that what appears to be imperfect bonding is in reality a more appropriate biological breeding system. There is a price to pay, however, for this flexibility. If males and females do not become totally, irreversibly bonded to their partners, then there is always a risk that one or other will become involved in a new relationship outside the pair. A new pair-bond may then start, creating a sexual triangle. This can easily lead to upheavals that harm the child-rearing process.

*Once it has reached a decisive stage, the human pair-bond is usually formalized by some kind of ritual. This demonstrates publically that a new, exclusive breeding unit has been established and must be recognized. The rituals take many forms, from highly elaborate marriage ceremonies to simple drive-in weddings.*

It would be reasonable to question why evolution has not adjusted the human pairing mechanism, so that loving pair-bonds can be weakened and broken only by the death of one partner. This would avoid wasting the reproductive potential of a solitary, surviving partner but would also give full protection to the children as long as both parents remained alive.

The fact that so many paired adults indulge in infidelities therefore requires some additional explanation. If the bonded pair are still together, why should either of them want to stray? What is the biological explanation of the passionate affair? The answer to this question can best be found by considering the two sexes separately.

For the male there is an obvious genetic advantage in carrying on both types of sexual activity at the same time, providing his casual affairs do not interfere with his role as a pair-bonded 'family protector'. To understand this, it is necessary to look at the two basic sexual strategies of animals.

The first strategy is to produce as many young as possible and to scatter them as widely as possible. This type of male mates with female after female. He never takes the slightest interest in his offspring, leaving that to the females in question, or simply to chance. Out of the many offspring he fathers, only a few survive – because they are so unprotected. But that is enough to carry on his line. This is the 'quantity solution'.

The second strategy is to produce very few young but to give them as much care and protection as he can. This is the 'quality' solution. He would have more offspring if he could but looking after too many would put them all at risk, so he concentrates on just the number that he can manage efficiently.

He may try to take care of his brood by himself. In some species this is the rule. But in most cases he is joined by the female to provide a double protection. With both parents giving food, warmth, shelter and defence against predators, these offspring have a much higher chance of survival. Again, the system works well.

But what if the good father, when out searching for food for his family, spots another attractive female? He has plenty of sperm, so why not present her with some? If he succeeds and she produces offspring, he will not be there to help them. His time will be completely taken up with his original family. But perhaps she will be able to rear them without his help. She might do this on her own, against the odds, or she might pair with some other male and let him bring up the offspring that are already developing inside her body.

For the male, this double strategy seems ideal. He carefully protects a few low-risk offspring and randomly sires other, high-risk offspring, a few of which may survive and pass on his genes. He gets the best of both worlds.

Returning to our own species, what is wrong with this solution? For the male, the problem lies in the potency of human pair-formation. If he could father extra children without becoming emotionally involved, either with them or with the extra females in his life, he would benefit genetically. He would pass on more of his genes to the next generation. But for human beings it is not that simple. As already mentioned, it is with good reason that we refer to copulation as 'making love'. The excitement of shared sexual activity automatically starts to create a new bond of affection. The casual fling can easily grow into a new pair-bond, even when this is the last thing that either partner intended.

Once a new bond has begun to develop, it clashes with the old one. Because the pair-bond is essentially an 'exclusivity device', there is no simple way out of such a conflict. Someone, possibly everyone involved, will suffer.

Sharing partners might seem a rational solution in such cases. This has been attempted from time to time, most recently in the communes of the 1960s and 1970s. They worked for a while but soon fragmented. Despite the best of intentions, passionate rivalries developed.

Even the most carefully planned and controlled communities based on sex-sharing did not survive for long. Perhaps the most successful was the bizarre Oneida community which settled in New York State in the 1840s. Dominated by a religious fanatic who also happened to be a sexual athlete, its members all lived together in one large building – the Oneida Mansion House, which still stands today – and where everyone was expected to copulate with everyone else. This sounded fair enough but there was a catch: the leader of the group awarded himself first choice of the young girls, while the younger men had to make do with the older women. As a result, it was the leader who fathered most children. In the 1870s there was a rebellion and the leader fled. By the end of the decade the colony had collapsed. Nor was this final rebellion the only problem the group faced. Throughout its brief history, it was repeatedly disrupted by forbidden romances and personal attachments.

Sexual jealousy has often been described as a wasteful emotion but it has a powerful place in our evolutionary biology. Its roots lie in the need to protect the offspring of the mated pair. Because our young are so demanding and because the parental burden is greater for our species than for any other animal, there is strong pressure to provide maximum security for the growing offspring in the family unit. This can best be achieved by ensuring that both parents devote themselves exclusively to their own brood. Any form of sharing threatens this priority. The evolution of intense feelings of sexual jealousy in our species has been one of the basic mechanisms for maintaining this system of maximum parental care.

An exception to this rule is the harem. When one male becomes so dominant that he can offer ample security to a large number of offspring, he can afford to inseminate a large number of females. In theory this should work well enough for the harem-master because his genes are assured of the safest of passages to the following generations. It does, however, involve two serious instabilities. It leaves many males without females and those men, robbed of their sexual heritage, will always be a threat. And it requires that the females inside the harem must accept a common partner without dissent.

A glance at the events which occurred in the greatest of all the harems, the Grand Seraglio of the Turkish sultans, reveals just how flawed this breeding system proved to be in practice. There were endless intrigues and murders and the whole complex organization could only be maintained by a rule of terror. The standard punishment for women who

could not accept their role was to be tied in a sack weighted with stones and drowned in the Bosporus. The sacks were placed in a small boat that was towed out into deep water. There, it was capsized by pulling on special ropes and the helpless women were sent plunging to their deaths. On one occasion three hundred women – the entire harem – were drowned in this way, simply because the sultan of the day wanted to enjoy the fun of stocking up with new females.

In stark contrast, during one phase of the four-hundred-and-fifty-year history of the great harem, the females took control. During this century-long Reign of Women, the sultans were left to indulge in orgies of drunkenness and vice, while the women took over the affairs of state. At times, they virtually ruled the country.

In this period there were endless battles for power among the senior women, with savage feuds and countless murders. To retain their power, older women would organize increasingly bizarre debaucheries for their sultan, to prevent him becoming bonded with any particular new female. There was always a risk that such attachments would start to develop, because of the primeval human need to form pair-bonds, even among harem-masters. These bonds, creating influential new favourites, had to be crushed as quickly as possible. One way this was done was by scouring the world for the most exquisite virgins and presenting a new one to the sultan, day after day. He was also encouraged to engage in mass orgies, where female individuality was all but destroyed. A favourite routine of one sultan was to have all his women stripped naked and present themselves on all fours, whinnying like mares, while he moved among them, acting the stallion until he was completely exhausted. For new loves to flourish under such circumstances was almost impossible.

*When one male achieves a sufficiently high level of dominance he may be able to implement a harem breeding system. However, although the harem is a common device in many other species, it creates problems in the naturally pair-bonding human species. The image of the Turkish harem depicted here is a highly romanticized version of the truth.*

The sultan's sons, as soon as they were born, were con-fined in a building called the Cage. At puberty each was given his own harem but all his females were sterilized, so that he could not yet produce offspring of his own to rival the sultan's. If an accident did occur, the newborn was immediately slaughtered. From time to time, the sultan would send specialist stranglers to his princes' quarters, to kill any of his sons whom he viewed as a possible future inconvenience. By the time that they reached full adulthood, those princes who managed to survive were already half-mad. From this corrupted source a new sultan had to be chosen.

The picture that emerges of life inside communes and harems is hardly that of a happy, extended family. It is clear that, once the simple pair-bond is abandoned as the basic reproductive unit of our species, all kinds of problems arise. At best, there is little of the loving parental care that helps to mature stable, intelligent offspring. At worst, grotesque excesses occur. We appear to be genetically programmed for family life and are only at our peak when we follow that programming.

How can we reconcile this with the familiar double strategy of the human male – that of keeping a long-term, loving family unit, while supplementing it with brief, casual sexual adventures elsewhere. How can the male urge to 'scatter his seed widely' be satisfied without wrecking the crucial family breeding unit? If affairs lead to rival bondings and if sexual sharing systems simply do not work, what can he do?

One answer is to restrict his casual sexual activities to the realm of fantasy. He has the imagination to day-dream them, to enjoy them vicariously on the stage or screen, or to explore them on the written page. There is a wide range available to him, from soft romance to hard pornography. Whole industries have been built on this form of outlet.

A more drastic step is to copulate with prostitutes. Here he runs the risk of disease and disgrace but is safe from the hazard of forming a rival pair-bond. Typically, the encounter is so impersonal that it is impossible for any deep attachment to take place. As a 'seed-scattering' procedure it is, of course, largely symbolic but for some males it may provide a sufficiently satisfying outlet, allowing them to carry on their pair-bonded activities without major disruptions.

Another male strategy is what might be called callous seduction. In this the female is a casual acquaintance who is the subject of a cold-blooded attempt by the male to 'score'. She is more of a sexual victim than a sexual partner. The male approaches the whole encounter so cynically and deliberately that the risk (for him) of becoming emotionally involved is minimized. Immediately he has achieved his goal, he loses interest and switches to another victim.

At the extreme end of the seduction scale is what has recently become known as date rape. The male, having failed to reach his ultimate goal, pushes persuasion to the limit and finally resorts to a degree of physical force. Beyond this is the savage strategy of full rape.

To understand rape, it is necessary to distinguish two distinct types. These can be roughly characterized by the labels 'sadist rape' and 'soldier rape'. Sadist rape has little to do with sex. Essentially it is an act of domination and humiliation, performed by men, who, when caught, usually turn out to be miserable, pathetic, inadequate failures. To save their tattered egos they require a massive boost of super-dominance. To gain this they must inflict pain and acute mental suffering on a helpless victim. It is the defilement and gross subjugation of the female that is the goal, rather than sexual consummation. In other words, it is an act of pathological domination disguised as sex, rather than a sexual act of a violent kind. Underlying this is the fact that female victims of this type of rape are often killed, making them useless as carriers of the male's genetic material.

Sadist rape is the solitary kind so frequently reported in the newspapers. Soldier rape is an entirely different matter. This is usually a group activity, ranging from the local, so-called 'gang bang' to the more widespread, war-zone ravaging. When a group of males moves into a region where they encounter the helpless females of a defeated faction or nation, they frequently indulge in an orgy of systematic rape. The goal here, although it certainly involves domination, is primarily sexual. Many of the women end up pregnant and there is a sudden, massive genetic input into the local population by the intruders. This is 'seed-scattering' on a grand scale and has been taking place for centuries, wherever an invading horde has succeeded in overrunning the territory of some other culture. The young warriors who perform these atrocities are not psychopaths, like the sadist rapists. They simply find themselves in an alien land, where they feel no sense of social control, and their urge to spread their genetic material overtakes all other considerations. After the conflict is over, they return home to their wives and behave, once more, like caring family men.

Because human males are driven to express themselves genetically with these two contrasting types of reproductive behaviour, social rules have frequently been introduced to bias them in one direction. The direction is always the same: towards the caring family strategy and away from the seed-scattering. In most societies today, adultery, bigamy, polygamy, prostitution, seduction and rape are punished in various ways. Some punishments are confined to social condemnation but most are also a matter of law.

The gravity of the offence has varied from time to time and place to place. In some regions prostitution is legal, in others it is strictly forbidden. In still others it is officially forbidden but in practice is permitted. Adultery may be a crime or it may be merely grounds for divorce.

There has been a curious shift in attitudes towards seduction and rape. Today rape is considered a much more serious crime than seduction, which is seen as no more than a social indiscretion providing that no force is used. In ancient times the exact opposite was the case, seduction being viewed as a far more serious offence than rape. The reasoning of the ancients was that if a man seduces a woman, he steals both her mind and her body, whereas if he rapes her he steals only her body. There was therefore more shame in being seduced than in being raped and the punishment for the seduction of a married woman was much more severe than for her rape.

No matter how the details have varied, there has always been general disapproval of the seed-scattering of the human male. It will always happen, because of its genetic benefit, but it will always be opposed, because it is a threat, both to the betrayed, paired females and to the rival males whose partners may become involved. (Despite this opposition, a recent survey of British males suggests that sixty per cent of them will be unfaithful to their long-term partners at least once during their lives.)

So far the male position has been considered. But what of the female? The situation is different for her, because conception saddles her with an inescapable parental burden. Following pregnancy, the human male may stay on to become a loving father, or he may vanish into thin air, but she has no choice – apart from the trauma of abortion.

Since the male partner is perfectly capable of giving his paired female all the children she can manage, there appears to be no advantage to her in copulating with extra males and risking the collapse of the established family unit. At first sight this would only make sense in the rare cases where the paired male partners had become impotent or infertile. Yet many females do apparently copulate with additional males.

Like human males, they indulge in a double sexual strategy. They form loving pair-bonds and become intensely maternal, yet they, too, indulge in brief affairs. (The recent British survey mentioned above gives the figure for unfaithful females as forty per cent – smaller than the male figure but still considerable.) This cannot be described as seed-scattering, so what precisely is its biological advantage?

For convenience, the three people involved can be referred to as the wife, the husband and the lover. Recent careful studies have revealed an extraordinary fact, namely that unfaithful wives time their sexual activities to favour their lovers: without being aware of what they are doing, they increase their sexual activities with their lovers at the times when they are ovulating. In other words, they unconsciously favour the sperm of their lovers over that of their husbands. This suggests that, although the moment of ovulation is hidden from them, its imminent arrival must nevertheless make them feel a little sexier – just enough to drive them to seek extra rewards. Independent evidence to back this up comes from blood-typing studies carried out in America, where it emerged that ten per cent of the children tested had been fathered by the mother's lover rather than her husband.

The reason why wives take these risks so often and endanger their pair-bonds is that they are driven by their biology to attempt to get the best of both worlds. They intuitively seek out, as long-term partners, those males who impress them as loving, caring protectors who will make good fathers and providers for the future. In their lovers they look for other qualities, such as healthy, powerful male physique, exceptional intelligence, high status or youthfulness.

Youthfulness carries a special benefit because, on average, younger males will offer her younger, fitter sperm. Sperm, like human beings themselves, have a typical life-cycle. They grow, mature, age and, if not used, die. Because older males have a lower sperm production and usually copulate less frequently than young males, it follows that their sperm will be older when delivered to the female. So females are programmed to find a young male more sexually attractive than an old one, assuming there are no overriding differences in intelligence or status.

This is not an attractive proposition for the older male unless he has reached a condition of total impotence and sterility. It means he is going to risk devoting all his parental energies to rearing offspring that carry another man's genetic material. He needs some special form of defence against this. In all societies he is likely to work hard to reinforce the pair-bond by loving acts. He is also likely to keep a close eye on his female and to monitor her social encounters.

In some cultures he may take special steps to make sexual activities unpleasant for her. There are literally millions of women alive today who have had their genitals mutilated to reduce their sexual pleasure and therefore to reduce their sexual interest in men. This female circumcision is routinely done in twenty-five countries, in Africa, the Middle East and Asia. The current figure is said to be as high as seventy-four million women.

In the past, at times when males have had to be away for long periods, they have even gone to the length of fitting their females with locked, metal 'chastity belts' which made it physically impossible for them to copulate. In reality, these did little more than make locksmiths extremely rich.

We now know, however, that evolution also took a hand, in the form of what might be described as a 'biological chastity belt'. To understand how this works, it is necessary to look inside the body of a female who has just made love. In the past it was always assumed that when the male sperm were ejaculated into the female vagina, they all started swimming energetically towards the tiny egg deep inside her, until at last one of them made contact and fertilization took place. It now appears that this is not true.

What happens following ejaculation is much more fascinating than that. For the human male has not one but two different kinds of sperm. These could be described as the 'go-getters' and the 'blockers'. The go-getters are the traditional sperm that swim until they find the egg. The blockers stay behind and form a barrier. They twine their tails together and perform a rearguard action. Like customs officials, they inspect the passports of any new sperm arriving. If they are sperm from the same male, they are allowed to pass. But if they are from some other male, their passage is blocked, they are attacked and killed.

*The most extreme form of sexual restraint was the formidable chastity belt, designed to ensure faithfulness of wives when their husbands were away on the crusades.*

This new discovery reveals that the human male is protected from cuckoldry in a quite remarkable way. For several days after he has mated with his female and deposited his sperm inside her, she will not be able to become pregnant by any other male. In primeval terms, this meant that he could mate and then take off on a long hunt without risking that on his return his female, either by seduction or by rape, would be carrying a fertilized egg fathered by some rival male.

Young males, who could mate almost every day with their females, would never have anything to fear. Their dying sperm would be repeatedly replaced with fresh reinforcements. No foreign sperm would ever stand a chance, providing the hunters were never away from home for too long. But the situation changes for the older males. They, unable to keep up the high mating frequency, would eventually become vulnerable. Younger males could sneak in and deposit their sperm at times when their elders had not set up their own sperm-barriers of 'blockers'.

Once this has happened, it is the sperm of the 'lover' and not of the 'husband' that are in the favoured position. It is they which form the biological chastity belt. Now, when the husband returns to his wife, it is his sperm that will find entry difficult. But husbands have their own special defence against this obstacle. New research has revealed that the more time a husband spends away from his wife's side, the more sperm he ejaculates the next time he mates with her. What he is trying to achieve with this increase is a 'swamping out' of the lover's sperm. If they are attempting to block his path, he will overpower them with a massive ejaculate.

This is 'sperm wars' being played out inside the body of the double-mating female. The amazing feature of this battle is that it is carried out without the two males concerned having the slightest idea of what is happening and without there being any conscious control over the number of sperm ejaculated.

It is important to correct one possible misconception here. It could be imagined that the husband who has been away from his wife has simply built up a bigger unused supply of sperm than the one who has been with her all the time. But this is not the case. If, for example, two husbands each make love to their wives and then both wait for exactly two days before making love to them again, the man who stays close beside his wife will produce a smaller ejaculate than the one who has been away on, say, a two-day trip. The ejaculate of the male who has been absent may be up to three times the size of the one who has stayed at home. This has nothing to do with virility. Both men may have exactly the same number of sperm ready to be used but they 'parcel' them out differently. ('Separation makes the heart grow fonder' and, just to be sure, it also makes the ejaculate grow larger.)

While the males battle it out inside her body, the female is far from passive. She has several special devices of her own to favour one or other of the sperm-owners. She can influence the success of different sperm by varying the way she has her orgasms. If she has a single partner to whom she is totally faithful, she will show an orgasm pattern that increases the chances of conception. If, however, she has both a long-term partner and a lover, she can favour the sperm from her lover, not only by (unconsciously) timing her matings with him to match her ovulation time but also by (unconsciously) having her orgasms in a way that increases the retention of his sperm. Conversely, such a female can influence the orgasms she has with her long-term partner so that they reduce sperm retention.

These influences are possible because of the way in which the female orgasm helps to draw the sperm up into the uterus. If the copulating female experiences her orgasm more than one minute before the male ejaculates or more than forty-five minutes afterwards, she will reduce the chances of conception. If she has her orgasm within that special forty-six-minute period, she will increase the chances.

This explains three familiar features of human copulation: why the human female usually takes slightly longer than the male to reach orgasm; why the male is so excited by arousing the female to orgasm; and why the female may fake orgasm.

So, essentially what the typical unfaithful female is doing is selecting the best genetic male for fathering her offspring, while selecting the most caring partner for her long-term relationship. The most stable pair-bonds will obviously be those where the male wins on both counts and the female needs look no further for her reproductive fulfilment. It is worth remembering that such couples are numerous and represent the peak breeding condition for our species. Only where this condition is in some way imperfect will the deceits of infidelity become evident. Society will always frown on such deceits but it is worth trying to understand the biology that drives them and the way in which couples attempt to perform the difficult juggling feat of keeping their family unit intact while at the same time maximizing their genetic success.

For the vast majority of humans, then, sexuality takes the form of heterosexual pairing and the establishment of a breeding family unit, accompanied by a certain amount of extra-family sexual activity. In our mainstream cultures, approximately ninety per cent of the population will follow this pairing pattern and about half of those will eventually, at some point, participate in extra-pair copulations.

In the early days of the human species, rapid breeding was important as our ancestors spread out to cover the globe. Today, heavily over-populated, the situation has changed. Non-breeders such as monks, nuns, priests, homosexuals, bachelors and spinsters are all valuable as non-contributors to the human population explosion.

There is, however, quite a large minority today that steps outside this ancient pattern and establishes a different lifestyle which denies the reproductive cycle. These non-breeders are most common in large, urban communities where the population density has soared to startling new heights.

Celibates, bachelors, spinsters, eunuchs, monks, nuns and homosexuals are all valuable non-contributors to the population explosion that threatens to destroy our species. Because they leave no children behind them, their blood-line stops with them and their genetic influence on their species vanishes as soon as they die.

It is no accident that, as human overcrowding has worsened year by year, homosexual behaviour has become increasingly tolerated by heterosexuals. Earlier attitudes, which saw homosexuality as 'sinful' and 'perverted', and made it unlawful, are now changing. For many people, hatred has been replaced by sympathy. In the popular mind, homosexuals may still not be fully accepted but they have at least graduated from being 'wicked' to being somehow 'sexually disabled'. This has dramatically reduced the levels of persecution that they have had to endure in the past.

In any other animal a non-breeding adult would have to be counted as a biological failure, contributing nothing to the history of their species, but with humans this is not the case. With us, there is always the possibility of a lasting, non-genetic influence of some kind. Many non-breeding individuals pass on a cultural legacy, through their works of art, their scientific discoveries and other such achievements. So all is not lost, even if they have stepped outside the genetic sequence.

There have been many arguments concerning the cause of homosexuality. If, as described earlier, there is a complex set of gender signals to which we are attuned as a species, then how can this crucial breeding system misfire so dramatically? How can our primeval urge to reproduce be misdirected so easily?

It has been suggested that there is a 'homosexual gene' and that homosexuality is a pattern of behaviour with which certain individuals are born. The folly of this argument is that any gene that reduces reproductive success will, inevitably, destroy itself. It is much more reasonable to suppose that there is something in the personal histories of homosexuals that accounts for their sexual preferences.

It is important to realize that there are two different aspects to homosexual behaviour.

First, there is the use of a member of the same gender as a partner simply because of the absence of the opposite sex. Sailors at sea for long periods, criminals confined to prison and schoolchildren in unisex boarding schools may all engage in homosexual acts on the basis that they are 'better than nothing'. When returned to the ordinary, social world, they quickly revert to heterosexual activities.

Quite distinct from such individuals are those who actively prefer the same sex, even when the opposite sex is readily available. In extreme cases they are quite incapable of interacting sexually with the opposite sex, even when attempting to do so. They have no choice but to form same-sex pair-bonds and establish themselves as pseudo-family units, often adopting animals as substitute children, as a way of satisfying their unfulfilled and unfulfillable parental urges.

Such individuals have usually experienced some kind of sexual mal-imprinting during childhood. When we first experience sexual sensations at the start of puberty, one of two things happens to us. We either gain our sexual awareness in a vague, gradual way, little by little, or it arrives as an intense, memorable moment. If there is a particular something or someone present during a sharp, intense awakening, then we have a tendency to become imprinted on that special feature. We endow it, or them, with a powerful sexual significance. If, as so often happens, we are sexually inhibited and shy at this early stage, then the special feature of our first, unforgettable experience looms larger and larger in our imaginations until we become fixated on it.

This is the background of many of our sexual oddities. All fetishists seem to begin their sexual histories in this way. If their initial arousals happened to be associated with objects made of leather, rubber or fur, then such substances may take on a super-sexual significance in later life. If the crucial element happened to be a member of the same sex, then that too would bias the subsequent, adult activities.

Social attitudes to all aspects of human sexual behaviour have varied enormously over the years. There have been permissive epochs and restrictive epochs, dissolute cultures and pious cultures, bawdy societies and chaste societies, hedonists and puritans, lechers and prudes. The pendulum has swung back and forth and has never come to rest. It is as though humanity has never been able to come to terms with its inherent sexuality. At one

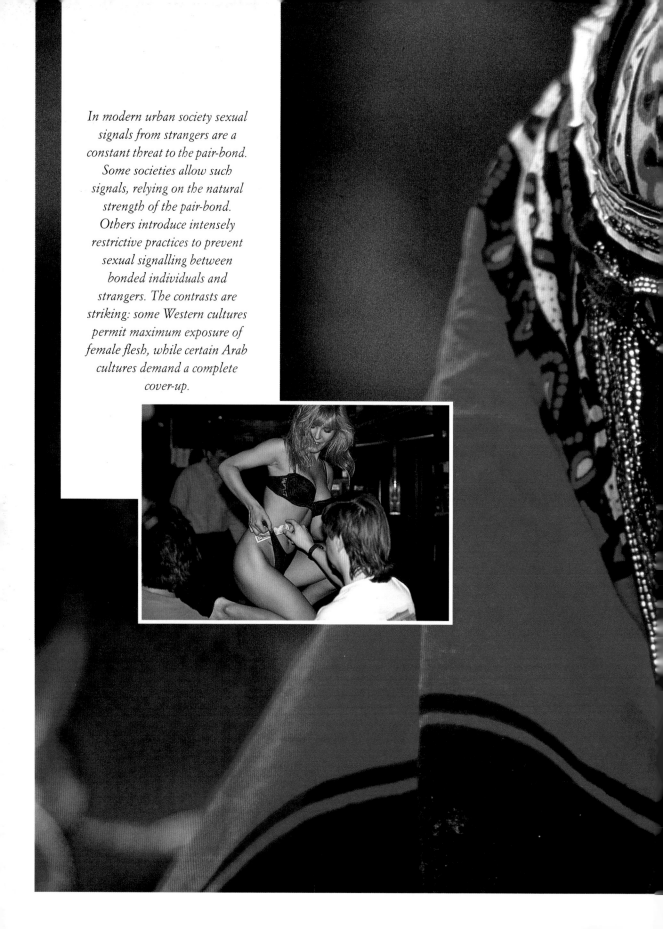

In modern urban society sexual
signals from strangers are a
constant threat to the pair-bond.
Some societies allow such
signals, relying on the natural
strength of the pair-bond.
Others introduce intensely
restrictive practices to prevent
sexual signalling between
bonded individuals and
strangers. The contrasts are
striking: some Western cultures
permit maximum exposure of
female flesh, while certain Arab
cultures demand a complete
cover-up.

moment it relishes and celebrates it, at the next it condemns and persecutes it. Frequently it does both at once, with breathtaking hypocrisy, living the social lie of a sexual double standard.

Why should there be this contradiction and confusion? The answer lies deeply embedded in the human success story. Our sexuality evolved during our long, primeval period of tribal hunting, when we lived in small groups where everyone knew everyone else. There, it made sense, providing a system of intense, erotic rewards which helped to keep breeding couples together.

With the increase in group size, however, a special problem arose. When tribal man became urban man, he was forced to encounter strangers every time he set foot outside his front door. These strangers displayed their sexual signals to individuals they did not know. They did not set out to do this but they could not help it. The shape of their bodies, their movements and their expressions did it for them. There was no appropriate response for this. Evolution had not equipped us to deal with all this random sexual signalling. We had to learn how to deal with it. That is why the system is so unstable and why it swings first one way and then another.

Some cultures reacted by becoming extremely suppressive. Clothes were worn of a kind that totally eliminated all sexual signals. Many Arab women are only allowed to appear in public submerged in shapeless costumes and with even their faces hidden behind masks and veils.

In other cultures women were not allowed outside the home at all. In some Mediterranean regions it was said that a woman only left her house three times: once to be born, once to be married and once to be buried. In many less extreme cultures, where a woman was permitted to appear outside her home, she was never allowed out on her own. She would always have to be chaperoned.

In Western cultures these restrictions have been greatly relaxed but this has put the pair-bond under increasing pressure. The presence of attractive members of the opposite sex in work contexts leads to endless sexual complications. The fact that their roles are non-sexual does not eliminate the powerful human sexual responses. This requires artificial, learned controls, which frequently fail to work.

In modern times human sexuality has therefore become a delicate balancing act. On the one hand, we all want to display ourselves as sexual adults – for the benefit of our existing or future partners – but on the other hand we do not want to attract all the members of the opposite sex whom we meet as we work our way through the day. We must send out sex signals but make sure that they are not too obvious. To back this up, we must surround ourselves with sexual laws and codes of conduct.

This is not an easy balance to achieve. If we allow our natural sexual urges too much play, we can easily find ourselves becoming social outcasts. If, by contrast, we suppress our sexuality too strongly, this too can be damaging. Many modern urbanites find themselves increasingly starved of simple physical contact and bodily intimacy. At moments when a hug or an embrace might be the appropriate, friendly reaction, nothing is done. Because we fear that our actions might be misinterpreted as sexual, we hold back. We do not touch, we keep our distance.

Self-imposed restraints of this kind can soon lead to psychological problems. Deep frustrations develop that eventually explode. For many, the need for intimacy finds alternative outlets. We stroke our cats and pat our dogs. And we find solace in solitary sexual gratification. Paradoxically, the more crowded our societies become, the more lonely it is possible to be.

For the majority, however, the ancient sexual patterns can somehow be successfully tailored to fit our strange, unnatural new world. We still manage to find a mate, fall in love, establish a pair-bond and rear our children. Our intense human sexuality may have been developed in simpler times but it has survived everything that has been thrown at it. Eventually, when our numbers have risen to impossible levels – as it seems they will surely do – we may have to face the extraordinary challenge of being forced to limit our breeding activities. The day may well dawn when we must all apply for a breeding licence before we will be allowed to procreate.

Whatever else may be said about our sexual behaviour, one thing is clear: of all our many behaviour patterns, copulation clearly remains one of our most successful and there are nearly six thousand million human beings alive today to testify to this.

# 5

# *The Immortal Genes*

There have been many arguments about the location of the immortal human soul. Could it be in the heart, in the head, or perhaps diffused throughout the whole body – an all-pervading spiritual quality unique to the human being? The answer, it seems to me as a zoologist, is obvious enough: a man's soul is located in his testicles; a woman's soul in her ovaries. For it is here that we find the truly immortal elements in our constitution – our genes.

These can be traced back to the beginning of life itself, each generation of genes recombining in a new, temporary housing, before moving on to the next step. Those temporary housings are, of course, us. Although we tend to see the world from our own point of view and marvel about our individuality and our character, as far as the genes are concerned we are merely disposable containers to house them briefly during their long march through time.

Why do the genes bother with us? Because, for them, we are a convenient way of maintaining some degree of flexibility. By juggling them around, courtesy of copulation, we keep their options open. We give them the chance of slight changes that will help them to survive a little better in an ever shifting world. Without us, they would become too fixed, too rigid, and could easily perish.

For them, the worst catastrophe is for us to fail to reproduce. If we do that, we are genetic disasters. The gene stops there. For every celibate – every bachelor, spinster, monk, nun and full-time homosexual, the failure to breed means that the millions of years of evolution that led to the ultimate formation of their sperm and eggs have come to a juddering halt. Their line is ended. Their potential immortality is no more.

For the rest of us, our children give us our genetic immortality. Our parents have handed on to us the chromosomal baton in the relay race of life and we have taken up the challenge by becoming parents ourselves. Ensuring that our genes continue without mishap in the new containers we have provided for them, we suddenly find ourselves overwhelmed by a desire to become loving, caring parents.

For most people, it is the arrival of their first-born that marks the moment when they begin to question the nature of human parental care – and the human life-cycle – but for me the moment came much earlier, at a time when I found myself acting as a foster-mother to a young chimpanzee. The infant ape treated me exactly like its parent and I began to feel strong parental feelings towards it.

So strong was the bond that formed between us that when, some years later, the chimp died, I experienced an acute sense of bereavement. There is nothing particularly unusual about this but for me it offered the chance of gaining some special insights into the unique features of the human infant. We are very close to apes, of course, but there are some important differences between the infant ape and the human baby. The one that struck me most forcibly was the difference in clinging ability. The little chimp clung to my clothing with a passion and desperation that left a lasting impression. It brought home to me the huge difference that arose the moment our ancestors lost their hairy covering. When the maternal ape became a naked ape (before the advent of clothing), it changed the whole relationship between mother and baby. As one of the higher primates, the human baby became uniquely helpless. And uniquely vulnerable. For it to be properly protected, the human parental urge had to be turned up to full volume. Humans had to become more devoted than any of their hairier relatives if their offspring were to thrive. The age of the super-parent was upon us — with all its magical rewards and its exhausting demands.

The human baby needs more attention – and for much longer – than the young of any other animal species. It was these special qualities that I began to study in detail when I began work on my book *Babywatching*. By looking at babies as amazing little animals and approaching them from a zoological standpoint, I was able to see them in a new way, and my earlier experiences as a chimp mother gave me a new perspective that I found invaluable.

As soon as I began to examine the way we behave with babies, I realized that there were still important lessons to be learned from our animal relatives. This starts even at birth. Other animals, for instance, give birth very easily. Human mothers do not. Why should there be this difference?

The common assumption is that the human female experiences a difficult, painful birth because her pelvis has to do two jobs. It must act as a birth canal but it must also support

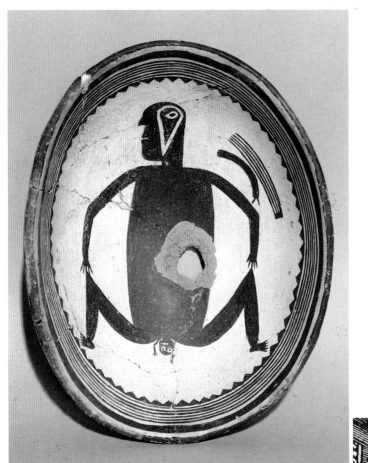

Ancient and tribal images of human birth show squatting as the natural posture. Even this Egyptian hieroglyph for birth depicts a squatting woman with the newborn's head and arms appearing from below her body.

A similar posture was adopted in earlier centuries in Europe, where the woman sat on a birthing stool (below), but in recent times all this changed.

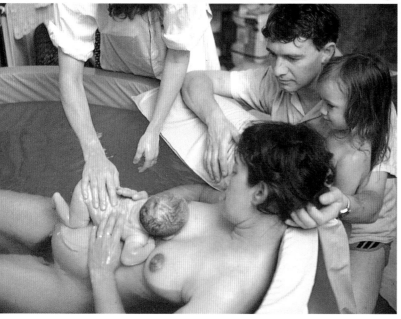

Hospital births required the woman to lie down and push, without the help of gravity, increasing the pain of labour. New techniques using birthing pools have greatly reduced the problems of delivery.

her vertical body. This conflict of interests has usually been given as the reason why she must strain and struggle to deliver her offspring into the world. Other, four-footed animals do not have this problem and can squeeze their babies out almost effortlessly, with a few simple contractions. But when our ancestors stood up on their hind legs and forced us to use our pelvic girdle as a support system, all this is supposed to have changed.

If we accept this explanation, then the human female will always be condemned to long and arduous labour. There can be no escape, except to reduce the extreme discomfort with various drugs and pain-killers. But is this explanation really valid?

From a zoological, rather than a medical point of view, it seems careless of evolution to have ignored this problem. A long and incapacitating birth process would have put prehistoric human females at a huge risk. It seems much more likely that somehow, today, we are doing something wrong and that human birth can be just as easy as that of any other species. What could have happened?

To find the answer, it is worth looking back at the way in which births took place in ancient times. The event has been recorded for us in many early works of art and they all have one thing in common. The mother is always depicted giving birth in a squatting position. Even the ancient Egyptian hieroglyph for birth shows a squatting woman, with a baby's head appearing beneath her.

Turning to modern tribal women, we find the same birth posture. Anthropological film of a tribal mother giving birth shows her squatting down on some large leaves and then gently delivering her baby beneath her, with the minimum of fuss.

Despite this, in modern times it has become the norm to require the mother-to-be to give birth lying on her back, as if she were a sick patient instead of a healthy woman performing a natural function. The medical mystique of the hospital seems to have overpowered the common sense which says: use gravity to give birth. Doctors lie the woman on her back and then shout 'push, push' at her, encouraging her to expel the baby horizontally.

Recently, the more advanced hospitals have abandoned this strange practice and allowed the female to adopt any posture she wishes. Those who are not afraid to experiment have found the squatting position much less effort. Some have gone one step further and have opted for a water-birth. In this, they squat in a birthing pool – a large container of warm water – and the baby is born beneath the surface of the liquid. This supports and relaxes the mother and makes the moment of birth even easier.

Providing the baby is brought gently to the surface without delay and then held to the front of the mother's body, there is no risk of drowning. The umbilical cord attaching the baby to the mother still supplies blood for several minutes after the moment of birth and the baby will not attempt to breath air until it has surfaced. This method of giving birth is growing in popularity, not only because it is so much easier for the mother, but because the baby also seems to benefit. Instead of suffering the trauma of being thrust directly out into the air, it goes through an intermediate stage, the warm water being reminiscent of the womb. It meets its new world in two gradual stages, instead of one dramatic one.

Some doctors are now insisting that a change in birth posture is not enough. There should also be a rethinking of the birth environment. It has been traditional for birth-rooms in hospitals to be treated like medical emergency rooms. There are bright lights, loud noises, shiny instruments and all the paraphernalia that is associated with illness and injury. All this, they say, should be changed. In its place should be dim lights – so as not to dazzle the newborn's eyes – soft and gentle voices – so as not to bombard its ears – and as little 'medical' atmosphere as possible – to reassure the mother. Again, many forward-thinking hospitals are taking these steps, with remarkable results.

For some mothers, even these steps are insufficient. They reject altogether the idea that birth should take place in hospitals (assuming all the signs point to a healthy, uncomplicated birth). Instead they opt for home births, where they can deliver their babies in the comforting familiarity of their own bedrooms. They argue that this makes them so much more relaxed that the births are much easier.

To some traditionalists, these changes seem unnecessary and there has been considerable resistance to them in some quarters. But to a zoologist they seem eminently sensible, because they focus on one thing – the comfort of the mother. There is a simple animal rule where giving birth is concerned: the more anxious the mother-to-be, the longer she takes to give birth; the more relaxed she is, the quicker she gives birth.

There is a good reason for this. When an animal gives birth it is vulnerable. Predators prowling around can pounce on her at this vital moment and she is helpless to run away. So, for most mammals it is crucial that the mother does not give birth until she feels completely safe. If she senses danger, special chemicals flood her body that instantly put the brakes on the birth process. Some species can delay giving birth, not for several hours but for several days, if they are uneasy.

This system has no meaning for human females today – they are no longer at risk from prowling lions or wolves – but they have not had sufficient evolutionary time to rid themselves of the ancient system of birth protection. It is now nothing but a nuisance but they are saddled with it nonetheless. If they feel at all anxious, their body chemicals will send out the instruction: Stop! Do not give birth yet. This will delay the birth longer and longer, which in turn makes them more anxious, causing further delays, and so on, until eventually, as they strain and struggle in great pain, they manage to break the circle and give birth. All this can be avoided if only they can make themselves relax as the moment of delivery draws near.

The secret for this is to adopt the most comfortable posture – whatever that may happen to be for a particular female – and give birth in the environment which feels most relaxing – again, wherever that may be. If hospital makes a mother feel more secure, she will be better off there; if the home bedroom makes her less anxious, then that is better. Finally, if she feels more at ease in the presence of close family, her husband or intimate women friends, they should be with her. If her husband, or anyone else, makes her nervous they should not be present. There are no rules about this other than her personal comfort. This is the message we get by watching the births of other animals and it is one that can help women to avoid much unnecessary suffering.

Once the baby is born, something very strange happens. It stays wide awake for about an hour. Despite the exhaustion of having been squeezed down the birth canal, its eyes are open and it is staring at the world around it. Only after that first hour is past does it fall into a deep slumber.

This initial period, before the slumber sets in, is a vital stage but its importance has often been ignored. Traditional, old-fashioned practice saw the cord quickly severed, the baby whisked away, washed and clothed. Of course, if, in an old-fashioned 'push-push' birth, the mother was completely drained, she might well have been too weak to do anything except take a quick, reassuring look at the baby and then subside. But if she had experienced a less arduous delivery, and she was not interfered with by professional helpers, she would have found herself naturally wanting to cradle the baby in her arms and gaze lovingly at its face. While she did this, the baby would have gazed back and that first magical hour would have passed as a powerful bonding time between mother and child.

There are those that say this is fanciful and that newborn babies are insensitive to the world around them – that what they can see is only a blur and they are really quite unaware of the presence of the mother. This is not true. By careful observation we are learning more and more about the remarkable sensitivity of the newborn to its surroundings, especially to its mother.

Its vision is much better than most people imagine. It is true that objects in the distance are not clearly seen, but there is good focussing at distances of between seven and twelve inches (eighteen and thirty centimetres) – precisely the distance at which it sees its mother's face. It reacts most strongly to large, bright, curved objects that show some movement – again all qualities of its mother's face. In other words, it enters the world programmed to focus on and respond to the maternal image.

New studies carried out in Crete have revealed more details about the interaction between the mother and her newborn. It has now been proved that, even at the ripe old age of *fifteen minutes*, babies are capable of imitating the changing facial expressions of their mothers. This discovery has startled even those who already accepted that the baby is a sensitive being, and not merely 'a bald head and a pair of lungs', as one vacuous Victorian described it.

Clearly, it is important for the mother to be separated from her baby as little as humanly possible following the birth. Ideally, the baby should never be removed to another room but should stay near to her at all times. If this is done, she and the baby will quickly learn to recognize one another both by smell and by sound. It only takes a baby forty-five hours to learn to identify its own mother by her body fragrance, providing there has been no artificial separation imposed upon them. For the mother, the process is even quicker. If she is allowed to stay in close contact with her baby for only half an hour after birth, she will be able to identify it later by its odour alone.

The same is true of sound. It only takes a mother three nights before she can identify the crying of her own baby, even in her sleep. She will wake for her own offspring instantly

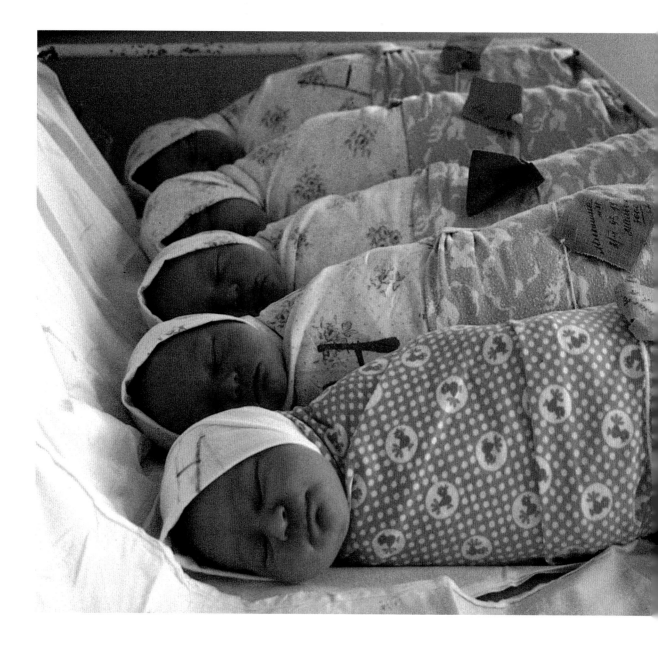

but not for the crying of other babies. And she has no idea how she can do this, or even that she has the ability if she lives in a house with only one baby present. This was clearly an ability that was appropriate back in our primeval days, when living in small tribes where each mother could hear at least several other babies in the still night air. To wake for them all would have robbed her needlessly of essential sleep. To wake to feed only her own baby was therefore important for her well-being and her survival. For its part, the baby can identify the sound of its mother's voice before the end of its first week.

It has recently been suggested that the importance of the close bonding that takes place

*Russian babies, swaddled and labelled, lie like a row of skittles in their hospital bed. Mothers only see them at feeding times and are allowed little free contact with them.*

between the mother and baby during the first weeks of the infant's life has been greatly exaggerated. One professor of psychology goes so far as to say, 'The bonding idea is a myth.' This argument appears to be designed to reduce the feelings of guilt of mothers who, for whatever reason, enjoy little intimacy with their newborn babies. The professor is honest enough to refer to her idea as a 'guilt-buster'.

That may be a kindly thought but more and more evidence is being collected proving conclusively that a great deal of subtle interaction – some conscious and some unconscious – is going on between the mother and child at this early stage. This sensitive interaction only makes sense if the bonding process is, indeed, a powerful one in our species. Why on earth would a human mother and baby have evolved the ability to identify one another personally by smell and by sound at such at early stage if there was no attachment process taking place? Guilt or no guilt, it is impossible to ignore the existence of bonding.

The extent to which mothers and babies are allowed to remain close to one another after birth varies enormously in different cultures. In two extremes – the simple, tribal cultures and the most advanced, Western ones – there is much closeness. Intimacy is encouraged. But in the less advanced urban cultures the scene is very different, and potentially damaging.

In a typical Russian hospital, for example, the newborn baby is quickly cleaned and wrapped and then whisked away to a nursery before the mother has had a chance to put it to her breast. In the days ahead it is returned to her only for brief moments of feeding. Finally, before she is discharged from the hospital, she is taken into the swaddling room where she is taught how to truss up her baby decoratively, like a Russian doll. This expert swaddling binds the infant so tightly that it is incapable of any movement. It makes little complaint about this treatment, presumably because the firm embrace of the swaddling clothes reminds it of the constriction it felt inside the womb during the final weeks of pregnancy. But although it may not cry when swaddled, its stiff immobility dramatically reduces the sensitivity of the intimacies it can enjoy with its mother – both for it and for her.

After she has swaddled her baby, the mother enters a ceremonial 'discharge room', where her husband and relatives are waiting for her. This is the first time the proud father will be able to set eyes on (what little is visible of) his baby. In this room the hospital atmosphere changes, as one Western observer put it, from that of an abattoir to an American funeral parlour. With stained glass and musak in the background, flowers are presented, family photographs taken and a voice announces, 'The baby is your dream and when you get home will grow up and take care of you'. Then they all leave. One can only wonder what impact this Russian birth routine must have on loving family life.

Most cultures have some form of ceremony that 'tribalizes' the baby and makes it a member of its culture. This varies from the harmless water rituals of baptism to the superstitious mutilations of circumcision. In all these cases the events proclaim the baby's arrival and its membership not simply of a family unit but also of a larger group – the society into which it will later become integrated.

For the baby, once it has settled into its new home, there is one overriding problem – attracting attention. Because it cannot cling on to its mother's fur like a baby chimpanzee, it must do its best to keep her near by other means. It can bring her running by an outburst of crying but once she is there, cuddling it, she must be encouraged to stay. In an ideal world, from the baby's point of view, mother would never leave. She would be in constant contact. But human mothers are busy and, unlike chimp mothers, must often carry out duties that make it impossible to stay close to the infant. So the infant carries on a non-stop 'campaign of appeal'.

Its greatest weapon is the human smile, a facial expression that is irresistible to parents and keeps them happily near at hand. The very shape of its head is also important. There is a strong parental reaction to what the Germans call the *kinderschema* or 'child-motif'.

The facial features of the infant stimulate a powerful protective response in human parents. The flat face, large eyes and snub nose all trigger inborn parental reactions. The same response is given automatically to many baby animals that show the same features and certain pets have been carefully bred to improve these infantile qualities, making them more effective as child substitutes.

This consists of several key elements: 1 large, round eyes with big pupils; 2 large, domed forehead; 3 chubby cheeks with a rounded jawline; 4 a flattened face with a small, snub nose; 5 a smooth, soft skin.

Together, these characteristics prove intensely appealing to the parental gaze. They make the mother and father want to stay close to the baby, pick it up, caress it, kiss it, talk to it and cuddle it. These actions all make the baby feel safe and secure. The bond between parent and child is further strengthened.

So powerful is this infant appeal that it can be exploited by cartoon artists who wish to gain our support for their characters. Examine the faces of any of the popular cartoon figures, from Mickey Mouse to Bugs Bunny, and you will find that the *kinderschema* principle has been liberally applied, with flatter, rounded faces being the norm.

The same is true of pet dogs. Small breeds that have been chosen as companions not only have the same body weight as human babies but also display the same large forehead, big eyes and flat face of the human infant. By selective breeding, their skulls have been gradually altered, their rough coats softened until they are silky to the touch and their natural, wolf-like behaviour made more puppy-like, increasing their dependence on their human foster-parents.

To some, these lap dogs are a travesty of the ancestral canine spirit but for modern urbanized humanity they are more appropriate than many of their larger, tougher, working-dog relatives. Modern city life is unkind to the old-fashioned, field-happy dogs, while the toy dogs and tiny companion breeds have come into their own. They arouse the same maternal feelings in their owners as do the actions, shapes and behaviour of real infants.

For centuries these small dogs have cheerfully taken on the protected role of child substitutes. In earlier times they were popular in royal courts and were exported all over the world as highly prized, princely gifts. In modern times they have become widely popular and play an important social role where there is human parental energy that is unfulfilled. For many owners with parental love to spare, they provide lasting solace, because, unlike real babies, they never grow up and they never leave home.

For the parent with a real baby, the process of growing up is both fascinating and a challenge. As each new phase appears, the subtle unwinding of behaviour patterns provides many intimate rewards. But there are also new problems. The parent must adjust to the rate of change of the infant. Sometimes a culture tries to rush its young ones too fast through the childhood stages and sometimes it tries to hold them back. Both errors can cause difficulties for the growing offspring but they are remarkably resilient and can usually make their own readjustments as time passes.

The first major phase is true babyhood. It lasts about a year and is characterized by the absence of both talking and walking. The baby may babble and burble but true speech is still in the future. This is the time dominated by sleeping and breast-feeding. Babies sleep twice as much as adults but break this sleep up into shorter periods, with feeding demands in between. Not until they are about six months old will they start switching to a pre-dominantly nocturnal sleep rhythm.

At this early stage, babies are impossible to train. They make their own rules and any attempts by parents to hurry them into imposed, fixed regimes are premature. This applies particularly to feeding. Because adults have more or less fixed feeding times, some mothers feel that babies should also be fed at set hours. The consequence of this is that there is a great increase in crying and considerable discomfort both in the mother's breasts and the infant's stomach. Neither is designed to deal with spaced out, large meals. Mothers who, instead, let their babies control the timing, and feed them on demand, find that the smaller, more frequent feeds suit both the baby and themselves much better.

During this phase some parents tend to distance themselves unnecessarily from their offspring. This does not happen in tribal societies but became popular in certain so-called 'advanced' societies in the twentieth century. The strict regime imposed on young mothers called upon them to place their babies in their nursery cots or their prams and leave them there for considerable lengths of time. If the infants objected with loud cries, these were to be ignored. The baby had to be 'disciplined'. This was a disastrous example of applying childhood control far too early. Schoolchildren can be disciplined, babies cannot. The results were insecure infants whose later personalities were harmed by this apparent lack of love during the first year of life.

Observations of monkey or ape mothers reveal that they would never attempt to impose such regimes on their offspring. When their babies are very young they receive total intimacy and love. Only when they are much older are they disciplined. This system is also appropriate for our own species. Babies that are breast-fed, frequently hugged and

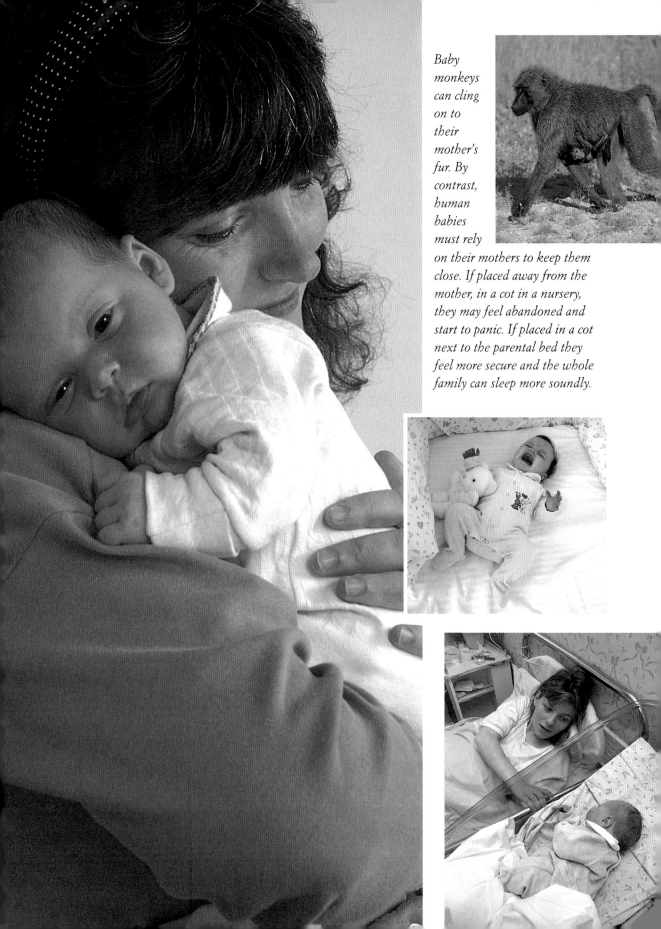

Baby monkeys can cling on to their mother's fur. By contrast, human babies must rely on their mothers to keep them close. If placed away from the mother, in a cot in a nursery, they may feel abandoned and start to panic. If placed in a cot next to the parental bed they feel more secure and the whole family can sleep more soundly.

cuddled, enjoy long play interludes with their parents and are isolated as little as possible are the ones that feel loved and therefore secure. Far from being softened or 'spoiled' by this treatment, they are in fact the strong ones, more ready to face the world.

Bearing this in mind, it is clear that the nursery and the pram are mixed blessings. It is unnatural for a baby to be left alone at night and it feels strangely abandoned. If placed in a cot next to its parents' bed, it will sense their presence and relax, crying far less and causing far less loss of sleep for all concerned. This is how young apes sleep – and probably how young humans slept in prehistoric times – and is a case where we can benefit by learning from our ancient relatives.

By the end of the first year of life, the baby has tripled its body weight and has started to walk. It has achieved this difficult, unique form of locomotion in gradual stages. At about seven months it can sit up unaided. By eight months it can stand up with help from its parents. By nine months it can crawl along the ground on all fours. Then from nine to twelve months it improves its crawling so much that it has to be carefully watched. Finally, and with much effort, it heaves itself up onto its hind legs and starts to totter along bipedally. By the time it celebrates its first birthday, it has already begun to master this extraordinary new mode of progression that we, as adults, take so much for granted.

The baby is now a toddler. Babyhood is past and an exciting new phase is beginning. The stronger limbs make all kinds of new play patterns and interactive games a possibility. Single words are blurted out and understood. Gradually talking develops. Fifty per cent of infants will have uttered their first word by the age of twelve months, ninety per cent by eighteen months. By the end of the second year, they are making simple sentences and the amazing human speech communication system is off and running.

The rate at which toddlers acquire their vocabularies varies slightly from child to child but a rough guide is: three words at twelve months, nineteen words at fifteen months, twenty-two words at eighteen months, 118 words at twenty-one months and 272 words at twenty-four months. There is clearly a big jump in word use in the second half of the second year of life. This is not purely a matter of learning. Toddlers are programmed to start speaking at this stage, regardless of how little encouragement they get. If parents are too busy to spend much time chatting with their offspring, they may slow down the process but they cannot stop it.

When they are two, toddlers have grown to the point where they are half their adult height. Their manipulation skills are advancing rapidly. They can handle toys, and simple feeding and drinking actions are mastered. This is a dangerous period because they are becoming much more mobile and are often stubbornly defiant of attempts to stop them investigating the world around them. Curiosity is intense at this stage and the new challenge of eagle-eyed parental protection has to be faced.

In the months that follow the second birthday, the young human begins to display a powerful ego. It has discovered the triple power of mobility, manipulation and speech, and its demands are heavy. Frustrations, stemming either from its own shortcomings or from parental attempts at restraint, frequently result in temper tantrums. In the human animal, egocentricity precedes cooperation.

By the age of three, the average child has a vocabulary of a thousand words and enjoys speaking so much that it can often be heard talking to itself. Its actions are becoming more dextrous and it is just starting to indulge in social play, although objects – and parents – are still more interesting than other children.

Typical four-year-olds know fifteen hundred words and are at the human peak of curiosity. Endless questions are asked, as the toddler learns more and more about itself and its environment.

The five-year-old knows two thousand words and is now ready to begin a decade of learning. Its brain has now reached ninety per cent of its adult weight and has to be programmed with all the information it will need as a young adult. The long educational phase from five to fifteen is the sponge or blotting-paper phase of the human life-cycle. Information is soaked up at an astonishing rate. Evolution has delayed adulthood while this happens. It has stretched out the childhood stage much further than in any other species.

During this period, reading, writing, drawing, painting, calculating and collecting all blossom. It is also the time when, regardless of parental attitudes, a strangely sexist attitude develops, with groups of boys separating themselves from groups of girls. Gang loyalty becomes important. Sport, humour and logical thought become significant pre-occupations, as does the pursuit of novelty. Intense friendships are also a feature of these long school years.

The predominantly uni-sexual nature of this phase is important because it helps to reduce the familiarity of the opposite sex. This sets the scene for the later, sexual phase, when a new type of relationship must be built across the gender divide. Any strong pre-sexual familiarity creates a 'brother–sister' type of relationship which works against the formation of a new sexual bond.

This childhood phase comes to an end with the delayed arrival of sexual maturity. By the age of fifteen nearly every girl has menstruated and has started to develop rounded breasts; nearly every boy has experienced a first ejaculation and most have also undergone a deepening of the voice. The sexist separation of schoolboys and schoolgirls into distinct social groups begins to fragment. Pairs form and, unless it is prevented by social custom, copulations start to occur.

The adolescent phase is a difficult one. Biologically, human beings become adults between the ages of thirteen and fifteen but legally they do not become adults until they are eighteen. And socially they are really not looked upon as adults until they are twenty-one or have settled into a job of work. This gap, in modern society, between the arrival of sexual urges and the arrival of social adulthood creates many problems. It becomes a turbulent emotional phase in the human life-cycle and one where parent/offspring relations are often strained to the maximum.

Because our complex societies demand ever greater levels of education, there is an overlap between the education process and the sexual one. Where the sexual urge over-powers the restraints of society, the result is the bizarre situation of young mothers still being viewed as schoolchildren. In certain areas this has led to the setting up of special schools, where breast-feeding can be fitted in between school classes.

When this difficult teenage phase is left behind, work becomes the main preoccupation during the twenties. All growth processes have stopped by the age of twenty-five and, physically, this is the peak moment of human life. Between twenty and thirty is also the most efficient time for breeding, with twenty-two being the 'age of fecundity', when the human female has her best chance for avoiding the death of her unborn child. The best age for giving birth, however, comes a little later, at the age of twenty-seven, when her baby is most likely to survive the trauma of being born.

During their twenties most people will have formed pairs and set up homes for themselves away from parental influence. With the arrival of their own children, the cycle begins again. The immortal genes now rely on this new generation of parents to protect and rear their fresh young 'containers'. To do this successfully, these new guardians must somehow divide their time between direct parental care and achieving the personal success that will provide them with a secure home life.

This balance is not always easy to achieve. If the parents devote too much time and effort to the workplace, family life may be neglected. But the most creative and inventive phase of the adult life-cycle happens to come in the late thirties, in the period when their young children usually need the greatest parental attention. It is in their late thirties that most adults will make their mark on society – if they are to make any mark at all. It is the age when they have spent enough years building their careers and gaining experience but are still young enough not to have become rigid in their thinking. (The age when most new inventions and discoveries have been made is thirty-eight.)

For many people today, reaching the age of forty causes an inexplicable state of anxiety. The buoyant, confident optimism of the thirties is exchanged for dark thoughts about the ageing process. It precipitates what has been popularly called a midlife crisis.

As they enter their forties, those who recently saw themselves as 'young and virile' suddenly fear that they have become 'middle-aged' and are losing their sex appeal. As a result they begin to indulge in romantic escapades with younger members of the opposite sex to prove to themselves that they are still capable of displaying youthful vigour. The level of career success that they have achieved by this stage of their lives is almost irrelevant here. What they are fighting is not a status battle but the ageing process.

There is a biological reason why this emotional chaos should reign for the early forties. There is a genuine decline in condition at this age, both physically and sexually. The catch is that there is not an equivalent mental decline. So the fortyish adults still feel mentally young and are alarmed to find themselves looked upon as now belonging to 'the older generation'. Tonics are sold that 'fortify the over-forties' and over-the-hill crooners declare that 'life begins at forty', as though replying to someone who has dared to say it stops then.

There is a serious risk that the compulsive lechery that explodes in the early forties will endanger the smooth ride of the immortal genes. If pair-bonds collapse as a result of the fall-out from the midlife crisis, and families break up permanently, any children involved may suffer. What they see may well deter them from repeating their parents' mistakes and the genetic line may be broken.

Curiously, the midlife crisis vanishes in a few years. Pair-bonds that manage to survive it may even be strengthened by it – because they have demonstrated that they are capable of withstanding almost anything that can be thrown at them. Couples that stay together into their fifties have a much better chance of remaining together into old age.

It may sound a harsh question but it is worth asking why, biologically speaking, anyone should survive after they have left their forties behind. Human females cease to breed in their early fifties. The menopause usually arrives between the mid-forties and the mid-fifties, with fifty-one as the average age. (The oldest age at which any human female has become a mother, without special medical aid, is fifty-seven, and that is exceptional.) Males are also in sexual decline and by the end of their fifties, twenty-eight per cent of them are impotent. So why do they hang around, taking up space, with an average life-span today somewhere in the early seventies?

There are two answers to this. First, if they are still breeding in their forties they need time to rear their last offspring. And second, they are needed by the immortal genes in a special role – that of grandparents. This is a uniquely human phenomenon and is a reminder that we have the greatest parental burden in the animal world.

To put this into perspective: some animals need perform no parental care at all. They simply shed thousands of eggs and sperm and leave the young to make their own way in the world. Enough survive to keep the genetic line going. One step up from this sees a mild parental burden that only involves the female. She looks after her young for a brief period. The young are not very demanding and grow quickly. Soon they are independent. Another step up sees the young too great a burden for the mother alone. The father must also help if they are to survive. A pair-bond is needed and a family home in which to rear the young. This is the human condition but even that is not enough. Because of the heavy workload that falls on the young, breeding adults, the offspring can benefit greatly from additional protection and care. That is where the grandparents come in. The children carry their genes, too, and they feel massively protective to the new toddlers in their lives.

For that reason alone, the unusually long life-span of the human species makes sense. But that is not all. There is a further reason for the existence of 'tribal elders'. In any tribal society without writing, it is necessary for someone to act as the protector of knowledge. Before there were books and written records, the old people in each group acted as the 'tribal libraries', retaining and retelling the tribal legends and myths, the history and the special skills. It was not necessary for everyone to attain an advanced old age but at least a few of these wise old men and women were needed in each group for the sake of cultural continuity.

Today this role of 'custodian of the tribal knowledge' has been usurped by modern technology. With books, films, tapes and computer print-outs we have rendered the 'wise old ones' obsolete. With the fragmentation of urban families, even the grandparental role is under threat. As a result, the high status of old age has suffered seriously and today we see old people not revered in the way they must have been during prehistoric times – when just to grow old was quite a feat – but segregated from the rest of society and confined to institutional 'homes for the elderly'.

*Grandparents who are past breeding age nevertheless have an important biological function in the human species, providing additional childcare that eases the prolonged parental burden of the mother. This explains the unusually lengthy life-span of our species.*

The irony is that modern medicine makes it possible for more and more adults to reach this elderly phase, while at the same time modern technology makes them less and less needed. A new role is required to replace the old one that they have lost but to date nobody has addressed this problem seriously.

Our greatest fears, as we pass the midlife mark, are of becoming ill and dying. When we are young we think little of such problems. Life seems to stretch out ahead of us for ever. We know we will die one day but it is so far away in the future that we do not give it a second thought. Then something happens – we are injured in a frightening accident, or a loved one dies or we see that our bodies are ageing visibly. Then, at last, we confront the issue and wonder what we can do about it.

This is a problem that other animals do not have. Uniquely, we are aware that one day we will die. This is an unfortunate side-effect of language. When we developed speech it was originally to tell one another about the present. But then we introduced tenses and the game was up. We did this to be able to talk about the past and use earlier experiences when solving new problems. It is this that gave us our great intelligence as a species – and

our past tense. But we also needed to plan, to work out what we were going to do on tomorrow's hunt. For this we needed a future tense.

The moment we could discuss the future we could contemplate our own mortality. For other animals, there is only the present. They are only concerned about dying when they face an immediate threat to themselves, right there in front of them. They react in several ways – by running away, hiding, withdrawing into their armour, squirting or injecting poison, stinging, erecting spines or attacking. At all other times they are blissfully unaware that one day they will become a tasty meal for some hungry predator, or will lie rotting on the ground.

For us, having contemplated death and disliked the idea, there was a need to find our own particular kind of protection. Because we could envisage it, we were, in a sense, permanently threatened by it and needed a major strategy to defeat it.

From ancient times we have found an answer: we conceived an 'afterlife'. We decided that, when we die, we do not cease to exist but instead move on to another place where we live for ever in a different state. Nobody has ever been able to prove or disprove the existence of this 'other world' but it has been a great boon to all those who can believe in it, giving them a hope that cleverly protects them from the fear of dying.

Some cultures, such as that of ancient Egypt, became so devoted to the idea of the afterlife that they put much of their time and energy into preparing for the great journey that they would have to undertake after death had claimed them. Inside their wonderfully decorated tombs, their carefully embalmed bodies were surrounded by all the trappings necessary for an affluent stay in the life beyond. Food, drink, clothing, furniture, jewellery, even servants and animals – anything they might need to make them feel at home – was entombed with the deceased. For the Egyptians, the other world was so real that it had none of the vague, ghostly qualities imagined by some other cultures. It was *this* life carried on somewhere else, and rather better.

On the walls of the vast, rock-cut tombs were depicted the various activities that the deceased hoped to continue to enjoy in the afterlife, such as feasting, hunting and sailing. Because it was feared the gods might demand humble physical labour even from the most exalted members of Egyptian society, and because this was unthinkable, small 'worker figures' called *ushabtis* (answerers) were modelled and included among the tomb goods. It was to be their duty to perform the menial tasks on behalf of their lords and masters. This would enable the Egyptian élite to enjoy an afterlife of eternal leisure. To ensure that there were enough labourers to last for ever, the *ushabti*-makers were asked to make more and more of these little figures, until eventually important tombs would have hundreds or even thousands of them standing by for their future duties.

Although the Egyptians took this to extremes, almost every culture on earth has had some form of burial service or cremation ritual to honour the dead and prepare them for their transformation. Because it was clear that the physical body itself rotted away, it was necessary to invent an immortal element that somehow escaped the dead carcass and soared safely away to its new life. This 'soul' was considered to be unique to human beings and lacking in animals. Some early sects which considered that perhaps animals too had souls were summarily slaughtered for such a blasphemous concept.

When Darwin arrived on the scene with his theory of evolution, this created something of a problem. Since it had long been established that animals did not have souls and since it now looked as though man was an animal, a crisis arose. Most people fudged the issue. Some said they thought that mankind had big souls and animals had small ones. Humans travelled first class to the Other World. Animals travelled in the hold – except perhaps for a few favourite dogs that were allowed to go tourist class.

Others sought a more scientific solution. They examined the nature of ageing and declared that it was not, after all, inevitable. It was simply the way in which the immortal genes ensured flexibility. This genetic material needs to turn us over, generation after generation, to retain the ability to change and adapt to the altering environment. Ageing was not, therefore, some cunning design of the Almighty but a simple biological mechanism – a built-in obsolescence. All that was needed to operate this was a gene, or a group of genes, whose instruction to the body was 'gradually decrease the efficiency of cell and tissue replacement'. That would slowly weaken us until we succumbed to one common ailment or another.

Once this idea is accepted, it becomes painfully clear that, one day in the future, with the aid of genetic engineering, we will be able to cancel out these 'ageing genes' and live for ever (assuming we are not hit by a passing bus). The snag is that we would rather like

to have this treatment now and it will probably not be ready for at least several generations. So how do we manage to stay around for that long? The answer, in a word, is cryonics.

Cryonics is the technology for preserving human bodies by deep-freezing them. It began as recently as 1967. The idea is that, by preventing decay in this way, a corpse can be stored indefinitely while medical science solves three problems. They are: finding a cure for whatever killed the stored body; finding a way of bringing the dead body back to life so that it can be cured of whatever killed it; and finding a way of undoing the damage caused by the crystal formation that occurs in the cells of the body during the freezing process.

*Because, uniquely, we were able to contemplate our death, we felt threatened by it. We allayed this fear by conceiving of an afterlife. To help us on our way there we provided special burial goods, including food and drink for the long journey. For the ancient Egyptians this became an obsession. Each society has its own way of dealing with death. The huge cremation towers of Bali provide a spectacular send-off for the deceased; the edible skulls of the Mexican Day of the Dead are part of an annual reunion with departed friends and loved ones; and in California the new technology of cryonics gives hope that deep-frozen bodies may one day be revived. The refusal to accept death as final is the driving force of all such activities.*

This may sound a daunting scientific challenge but it does at least offer a very slender chance, whereas burial or cremation offers the human body no chance whatever. For most people, however, the chance is too slender and the number of people who have gone to the expense of having themselves deep-frozen remains small.

What happens to that tiny, hopeful band is as follows. When they are dying they alert the cryonics technicians, who wait for the end to come. Then, ideally within ten minutes of death, the experts move in and replace the body's blood with a special preservative liquid. This has been developed to reduce to the minimum any cell damage. When this process, called cryo-protective pro-fusion, is completed, the body is taken to the cryonics centre and suspended upside down inside a large metal container. The container is filled with liquid nitrogen at minus 196 degrees centigrade. And there it stays, awaiting a future medical miracle. (The reason it is stored upside down is that, in the event of earthquake or civil disturbance that might prevent the technicians from topping up the level of the liquid nitrogen for months, the most important part of the body – the brain – would be protected longest.)

Because cryonics is the science of 'life extension' the bodies are not referred to as corpses or cadavers but as patients. They are stored, not in a mortuary but in a 'patient care bay'. For most people, this is too extreme a measure to contemplate but many nevertheless take some steps to extend their lives, if in a less dramatic manner.

These steps include improving mental condition or physical health in some way. Some doctrines insist that a 'healthy mind' is the clue to a long life and there is some evidence to support this. Studies that have looked at the personalities of people who live to be a hundred have revealed that they do, indeed, have certain attitudes in common.

The special qualities of the very long-lived, which they tend to show throughout their lengthy life-span, include the following:

1  They take a natural pleasure in regular exercise. They enjoy activities such as walking and gardening but in a relaxed way. They do not take vigorous exercise that is motivated by anxiety about health. Their physical exertions are extensive rather than intensive. They do them for fun rather than as a health duty.

2  They have a calm but lively personality. They have a zest for life but do not exhibit emotional extremes that give rise to outbursts of anger or moments of panic.

3  They avoid nostalgia. They do not live in the past. To do so is to contemplate times when they were younger, faster and stronger, and that can be depressing. Instead they live very much in the present, with enthusiasms for the activities of the day.

4  They are successful at what they do. This does not imply major success. Their goals may be very modest but if they achieve them, in their own eyes, this will act as a life-stretcher. In fact, the very long-lived are more concerned with what they *do* rather than with who they *are*. They are proud of their work rather than themselves.

5  They are moderate in their habits. They eat a varied diet that avoids all extremes. They consume a regular daily mixture of meat and vegetable food, and also take a moderate amount of alcohol. They live longer than those who suffer from what might be called 'food and drink anxiety', of the sort that leads to various kinds of self-denial. Equally, they tend not to be the gourmets who develop food and drink into an art form.

6  They have an ordered lifestyle. This does not imply a strict, military-style control. Rather, it suggests a daily routine that is free of chaos and stress.

7 They have a twinkle in the eye. A sense of humour survives with them even into extreme old age.

With these qualities it has been possible for some human individuals to live amazingly extended lives, making them the longest-lived mammals on earth. The current record-holder – for a fully authenticated human life-span – is Mr Shigechiyo Izumi from Japan, who died recently aged 120 years and 237 days. A saki-drinking, television addict in his later years, he gave his secret as 'not worrying'.

Many human beings have lived for as long as half a century after they have ceased to be able to reproduce. These long, post-breeding years may not have helped to contribute directly to the onward march of their immortal genes but they will have contributed indirectly in many ways.

Those younger individuals who wish to live long lives themselves can learn something from the centenarians. They can try to impose on their lifestyles the qualities that, to others, come naturally. But this has to be done in a gentle, cheerful way. If it becomes a harsh duty it will defeat itself.

Equally self-defeating are most of the health fads and diet regimes, the jogging and the gymnastics that many today use to create the 'perfect body'. There is little evidence to suggest that such individuals live longer than those who are more moderate in their restraints and exertions. All these more extreme forms of self-discipline are born out of deep-seated anxieties that are themselves the real killers.

Whatever happens to the individual life, so long as there are offspring to carry on the genetic line there will be a kind of immortality – a biological, genetic immortality. Despite the fact that we ourselves are not around to witness this, it remains the most important form of 'life extension' known on this planet. And unless we pollute the globe beyond all recognition, it will ensure the presence of our species here for a very long time to come.

# 6

# *Beyond Survival*

For most animals the struggle to survive takes up all their time. Finding food and drink, keeping warm and clean, avoiding predators, migrating and reproducing use up all their energies. If they do have any time to spare, they spend it resting or sleeping. Only very young animals, under the protection of their parents, have enough surplus energy to engage in lively bouts of play.

This was also true for our early ancestors. The constant search for food would have put heavy demands upon them. But as they slowly evolved into more and more efficient hunters, the situation changed. The secret of their success was the development of much greater intelligence. They used brain not brawn to kill their prey. At the end of the long hunting epoch, before they turned to farming, they were already enjoying some degree of affluence. In certain regions, at particular times of year, the prey was sufficiently plentiful and their hunting techniques sufficiently advanced for them to experience a remarkable degree of prosperity. They had time on their hands.

It was at this point that our ancestors became truly human and started to show a distinct difference from other successful species. When the pickings are exceptionally good for a pride of lions, for instance, they hunt quickly and efficiently, then spend the rest of the day sprawled out lazily digesting their kill. In a similar situation, our ancestors behaved in a new and special way. They may have enjoyed a snooze but they soon became restless. The big brains that gave them the prosperity also gave them an insatiable urge to keep active. Instead of ceasing to play when they became adults, humans retained that childlike playfulness and extended it into more serious, adult forms of play.

Today, we call adult play by many names. We label it under distinct headings, such as art, poetry, literature, music, dance, theatre, cinema, philosophy, science and sport. Most of these names were absent from the vocabularies of ancient peoples. They did not see them as separate categories. All adult play was woven into the lives of the people as part of their tribal existence. There were no specialists. Everyone was involved.

Then, with the growth of urban life, division of labour developed and specialists arose.

*Young lions and young humans are both playful, but when they become adult a major difference emerges. Adult lions cease to be playful, but humans do not.*

*When a lion has fed, it snoozes. Successful lions sleep twice as long each day as their human counterparts. Humans keep on playing, right into old age.*

As the various forms of playfulness became more and more advanced and sophisticated, it became increasingly difficult for ordinary people to keep up with the specialized skills. Now there were distinct careers for the expert artists, writers, composers, dancers, actors, and so on. Everyone else became, simply, the audience.

As the skills of the specialists have been improved from generation to generation, what we have witnessed has been the blossoming of the most extraordinary achievements of any species in the history of this planet. It has been so astounding that it has frequently overshadowed everything else.

Eventually it led us to the mistaken belief that we cannot possibly be animals. If we can paint masterpieces, build cathedrals and compose symphonies, how can we conceivably be compared with other species? There must surely be some mistake. We must have been put here, by gods or aliens, to look vaguely like other animals – so that we would fit comfortably into the planet's environment – but in reality we are outside biology.

It was this error that I set out to correct when I wrote *The Naked Ape*. I wanted to redress the balance and remind us that, no matter how extraordinary our achievements may be, we nonetheless remain animals and subject to all the usual rules of biology. If we ignore those rules and, for instance, overpopulate and pollute the planet, we will not be protected by some supernatural force. We will become extinct just as easily as any other species.

Because I emphasized the more basic, animal aspects of human behaviour, such as feeding, sex, aggression and parental care, I was accused by some as having forgotten mankind's crowning glories. This was not the case. It was simply that in the past we had sung our own praises so often and so loudly that I felt a balance was needed.

As it so happened, my first book *The Biology of Art*, published many years earlier, had been an attempt to trace the origins of the most ancient of all forms of adult play and to see how, from biological roots, the great tree of human art could blossom. The earliest evidence we have of this activity is a staggering three million years old. In 1925 a strange object was found in a rock shelter at a site known as the Limeworks Quarry in the Transvaal in southern Africa. It was a water-worn, reddish pebble that seemed curiously out of place. Investigations revealed that it could not have come from the cave where it was found and must have been carried from a location about three miles away. What made it special was that it had the shape of a human skull, on one side of which were small cavities that looked like a pair of sunken eye-sockets above a simple mouth. There is no suggestion that this 'face' had been artificially manufactured but its accidental resemblance is so striking that it seems certain the object was collected and brought back to a favoured dwelling place as a 'treasured possession'.

Known as the Makapansgat Pebble, after the site where it was found, it is thought to be

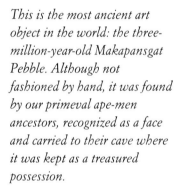

*This is the most ancient art object in the world: the three-million-year-old Makapansgat Pebble. Although not fashioned by hand, it was found by our primeval ape-men ancestors, recognized as a face and carried to their cave where it was kept as a treasured possession.*

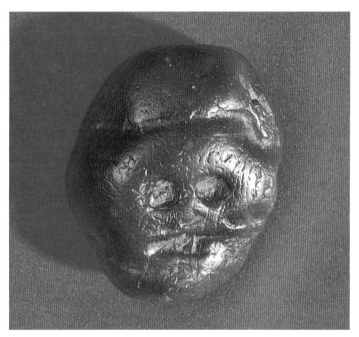

the most ancient art object in the world. What makes it so extraordinary is that the cave where it was discovered was not occupied by prehistoric man but by the early man-apes known as the Australopithecines. They may not have been capable of fashioning a model head themselves but they were at least able to see one in the natural surface-weathering on a pebble and to be so impressed by the image that they were moved to carry it home with them, over a long distance.

In performing this seemingly simple action of collecting an unusual pebble, those primeval man-apes were in reality taking a giant step. They were seeing a face that was not a face. They were reacting to something that stood for something else. By responding to the image on the pebble they were indulging in a primitive form of symbolism. They were struck by a resemblance, by an accidental echo, and were so fascinated by it that they carried it for three miles. This long journey, carefully transporting the pebble, reveals that their interest in the pebble-face was not a fleeting reaction but a serious preoccupation.

Fashioning an image, as distinct from collecting one, appears to have been beyond these man-apes, and was still a long way off in the future. Until recently, it was thought to be a creative act that occurred only in the last fifty thousand years of the human story. A recent discovery in the Middle East has now pushed that date back to three hundred thousand years, but even this is still quite young compared with the Makapansgat Pebble.

The newly found sculptural object – the most ancient man-made image in the world – is a small stone figurine of a woman, unearthed at an archaeological site on the Golan Heights. It is extremely crude, but the head is clearly separated from the body by an incised neck, and the arms are indicated by two vertical grooves, apparently cut by a sharp flint tool. It is a find that establishes the even greater antiquity of the human fascination with symbolic images.

*This is the oldest man-made art object in the world. Recently discovered in the Golan Heights and now in the Jerusalem Museum, it is a small figurine of a rotund woman fashioned three hundred thousand years ago.*

This acceptance of a 'symbolic equation', of letting one thing stand for another, has its roots in animal play. When a kitten pounces on a leaf and attacks it, the young animal is reacting to the object as if it were a mouse. In children's games the same kind of reaction becomes the basis of make-believe play. Once this process arrives at the point where objects are being made specifically to stand for other things, then a new threshold has been passed.

In the elaborate rock art created by the Australian Aborigines, we know that the artists felt that the animals depicted on the rocks actually lived in the rocks. The images, once depicted, had a magical existence of their own. They became powerful spirits and the locations where they were painted became sacred places.

In the tombs of ancient Egypt a similar intensity existed. The images on the walls were again felt to embody the spiritual force of the scenes they revealed. But here we see another stage in the development of symbols. About five thousand years ago certain images became stylized and simplified into hieroglyphs. These were then strung together to tell a story. It was only one more step from this to the development of a written language in which the

*For fifty thousand years the inhabitants of Australia have decorated and redecorated the surface of their rocks with strange images. Once a figure has been created it is believed to have a life of its own in the rocks, and its image must be re-worked at regular intervals to keep it strong.*

letters and numbers no longer bore an obvious relationship to the pictorial images on which they were based.

In the alphabet we use today, for example, modern letters can be traced back to Egyptian hieroglyphs of a recognizable, pictorial kind. The letter N comes from the zigzag shape of a snake; the letter E is a human figure with arms raised, turned on its side; the letter A is a bull's head turned upside down; and the R is a simplified human head in profile. But if I write these four letters down together – NEAR – their pictorial origins no longer have any significance. The original, direct symbolism has been lost during five thousand years of refinement.

EGYPTIAN ⟶ MODERN

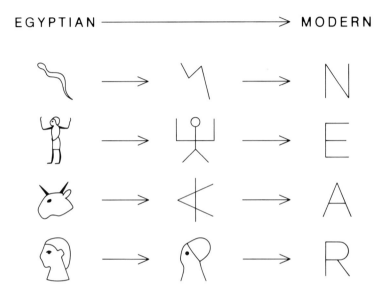

So today we have two kinds of symbols: the stylized and the unstylized. Stylized symbols operate on the basis of a convention. We may or may not be able to detect their origins but it does not matter. We all accept the convention of what they mean. We may or may not know why a circle above a cross stands for 'female' but we agree that it does. By contrast, the origins of unstylized symbols are always obvious. A painting of a landscape clearly stands for a landscape.

In the twentieth century this point was crystallized in one extraordinary painting by the Belgian surrealist, René Magritte. The picture shows a carefully, realistically painted image of a smoker's pipe. Underneath the artist has written the words 'Ceci n'est pas une pipe' – 'This is not a pipe'. Asked why he had contradicted his image in this way, Magritte replied 'Because you cannot stuff tobacco into that pipe'. In other words, although we accept it as an image of a pipe, it is in reality something flat, made of canvas and pigment.

Ceci n'est pas une pipe.

The ancient man-apes of South Africa knew that the face on the Makapansgat Pebble was not a face and yet it was a face. We today know that the painting of a pipe is not a pipe but we accept it as one as we look at it.

This use of the symbolic equation is the basis of all the games we play, all the story-telling, all the theatre and cinema, all the fiction, all the fantasy, mythology and legend, and all the pictorial art. If we cannot make that leap, from the real to the seemingly real, and – just for a while – respond to them as one and the same, then art has lost one of its main functions.

*The image we create is not the thing it represents. We may say of this picture 'it's a pipe' but, as the artist reminds us, it is not a pipe. Our ability to let one thing stand for another – the symbolic equation – has proved to be one of our greatest attributes.*

There is, however, much more to art than symbolism alone. Viewed from a different perspective, art is also concerned with decoration – with making things startling and

Art as decoration: when we want to make something more appealing to our sense of curiosity, we elaborate it. One of the most ancient forms of decoration was body-painting and adornment. Seen here in New Guinea (right), Kenya (main picture) and Brazil (below), it remains widespread even today.

For certain individuals, the decoration of the body must somehow be made more permanent – either by tattooing (above) or by scarification (right). By demonstrating permanent commitment to these types of transformation, we emphasize their importance to us.

unusual. It involves, as another of its basic functions, the transformation of the ordinary and the unremarkable into the extraordinary and the remarkable. It does this by decorating the plain, by amplifying the quiet and by exaggerating the modest.

Unadorned human bodies become intensely marked display-surfaces. Costumes and ornaments are added to amplify personal decoration still further. The drab surfaces of dwellings, utensils, weapons and vehicles become patterned and brightly coloured. Whole settlements become decorative works of art, exciting the eye and firing the imagination.

In most cases there is an attempt to create a strong contrast with the environment. This explains why so much of tribal art involves the use of geometric patterns. Countless examples of ancient pottery and tribal artefacts are covered in geometric shapes and lines. To us today these patterns may seem austere but to the artists concerned they must have been excitingly new and different – different, of course, from the organic world in which they lived.

In modern times, we live in geometrically designed houses and apartments, in geometrically designed towns and cities. Geometry is no longer a novelty for us. When we hang a decorative picture on our walls it is much more likely to be a landscape than a geometric pattern. In the world of the city-dwellers, it is the idyllic countryside scene that provides the startling contrast with their environment.

Like symbolism, decoration is a very ancient practice and can be traced back at least three hundred thousand years. At the ancient site of Terra Amata, in Nice in southern France, special pigment was used – on something or someone – to make them more vivid and colourful. We know this because seventy-five pieces of red ochre were found at this remarkably early site of human habitation. These pieces of ochre had been worked on and shaped by the prehistoric people who were living there in small oval-shaped huts. Clearly, by this stage of human evolution, red colouring was being employed for some special, decorative purpose. Indeed, it may have been both decorative and symbolic, serving both artistic functions at once.

Red colouring has always been favoured in works of art, all over the world, for the simple reason that it is one of the rarest of natural colours, contrasting strongly with the common greens and yellows of vegetation. To use red in decoration automatically makes it stand out against its background. Being the colour of blood and fire, it also has a powerful symbolic significance to add to its appeal.

It is not surprising therefore that red ochre was to be favoured again when, about thirty thousand years ago, Stone Age artists began their extraordinary work on the walls of the painted caves of France and Spain. The pictures discovered there, at the now famous sites of Lascaux in central France and Altamira in northern Spain, made nonsense out of the term 'primitive art'. The technology of the people who made them may have been primitive but the painted images themselves were anything but primitive. They showed a sensitivity and visual flair that shattered the popular conception of prehistoric man as a crude, violent, brutish creature.

The subject matter on the walls of the Stone Age caves was largely animal in nature. At first it was thought that the species depicted must represent the usual prey animals of the people concerned. The pictures, it was suggested, were educational, used in the training of young hunters. However, studies of the animal bones found in the debris of the floors of the painted caves showed that they did not match the pictures on the walls above them.

It is clear from the bones that the tribes of the cave artists were dining on many small animals as well as some large ones but only the big, important species were depicted in paint. It was as if the artists considered the larger species – the rhinos, horses, deer and buffalo – to be worthy of special attention, while the little food animals – the foxes, rabbits and other small mammals and birds – were suitable only for the menu.

It was suggested that perhaps the pictures were painted to gain power over the large animals to be hunted in the days ahead. This idea also collapsed when it was demonstrated, from the postures of the feet of these animals, that they were all depicted in positions of death. By taking photographs of live animals, standing on all fours, and also dead animals, lying on their sides in a slaughterhouse, it was clear that the angle of the feet in the prehistoric paintings matched the slaughtered specimens not the living ones. They were carefully depicted on tiptoe, a foot position that is common when a hoofed animal is lying on its side, as in death, but not when it is alive, with the weight of its heavy body pressing down on its small feet.

This discovery meant that the Stone Age artists could hardly have made their cave paintings from memory. They must have made sketches (perhaps drawn on dried skins) of the large animals that had just been killed, at the end of a hunt, and then taken these sketches back to the caves to be laboriously transferred onto the walls. It was as if the

artists were commemorating the animals killed and perhaps honouring them by giving them a new resting place. Perhaps, as they were painted, their killing was re-enacted and the moment of tribal triumph was celebrated in mime and song.

In other words, these prehistoric cave paintings were not guides to future hunting but memorials to the victims of past hunts. And, naturally, it was the bigger, more impressive animals that justified this special treatment, for in them lay greater danger and greater reward.

*The animals in the prehistoric cave paintings of France and Spain are so accurately portrayed that it is possible to tell from the position of their feet that they are depicted in postures of death. The hooves are extended and bear no weight. It appears that these paintings were commemorations of recently killed animals.*

There also appeared to be another factor at work. In some of the caves it was possible to show that certain kinds of animals were located in certain sections of the cave, as though there was some sort of ritual involved. The painted walls were not so much a reflection of daily life but rather a kind of 'mural bestiary'. There were often strange signs and markings alongside the naturalistic animal images and these suggest that something complicated was involved. We may never know precisely what was taking place, all those centuries ago, but it is certain that, whatever it was, a great deal of ritual, symbolism and ceremonial was involved.

With these cave paintings we come, for the first time in the human story, to a third basic feature of art, namely recording. What we today find so astonishing about the primeval paintings on the cave walls is their accuracy. The stylishly portrayed animals display elegant, realistic proportions. These are not crude symbols or mere decorations, they are precise representations.

Representational images are comparatively rare in the history of art. We think of them as commonplace because we are steeped in the European art traditions of recent centuries but viewed globally over the whole of human history it is clear that stylized, symbolic art is much more widespread and frequent. This is not a matter of skill but of preference. Art has been mystical more often than documentary, magical more than imitative, emblematic more than figurative.

The reason for the precision of the ancient cave paintings appears to be that it was important for the artists concerned to portray a particular animal in a particular posture. These were records of specific events rather than generalized portraits. In one instance an animal is shown with its entrails hanging out; in another there are marks indicating wounds – presumably fatal ones; in yet another the neck is twisted round awkwardly, as if broken.

Surprisingly, two things are missing from these cave paintings, namely, composition and reverence for the finished product. Sometimes composition may appear to be employed, with relations between individual animals having some significance, but this is almost certainly accidental. Each animal exists on its own, without reference to other elements. This is emphasized by the fact that in many cases one animal is painted over the top of another, as if the original picture has ceased to be of any interest. This obliteration suggests that the act of portrayal was linked to a particular ceremony or ritual event. Once this was performed, the picture eventually ceased to be of importance and could be over-painted without any sense of desecration.

It is clear that these most ancient of surviving human paintings are already highly complex, both in manual skill and social significance, and can tell us little about how our first fumbling attempts to create pictorial art began. Those artefacts are obviously lost for ever. The search for the roots of human art must lie elsewhere.

Instead of looking at the earliest art forms, an alternative approach is to look at the youngest. Child art offers another way of exploring the nature of aesthetics. By examining thousands of pictures painted by very young human artists, it is possible to observe the unfolding of the process.

In the earliest stages, when the child is very young indeed, between one and two years old, the hand and arm find it hard to exert accurate control on the lines being formed. The first scribbles show little organization. Before long, however, the scribbles become bolder and the two- to three-year-old child is capable of making vigorous marks on a sheet of paper. Soon, simple images begin to emerge from the tangle of lines. Remarkably, the process is much the same the world over, regardless of the cultural history of the children. Between the ages of four and five, all infants everywhere start to distil pictorial images and vary them.

This always follows the same pattern. From an analysis of two hundred thousand drawings made by young children it emerged that the initial scribble stage gives way to a 'diagram stage', when the mass of busy lines is reduced to a few simple units. These consist of such motifs as the cross, the square, the circle and the odd-shaped area. These grow, almost by accident, out of the early scribblings. They appear in all children and are not the result of adult teaching but of visual exploring.

The diagram stage is followed by the 'combine stage', in which the child starts to put diagram units together to make more complex motifs. It is from these that the first pictorial images emerge. The most common of these is the human form.

The human form nearly always develops in the same, rather strange way. It begins as a circle with blobs inside it. These blobs are then organized into eyes, nose and mouth. Lines radiating around the circle that forms the head represent the hair. Then some of these hairs become longer and longer, extending into arms and legs. At this point the figure lacks a body but one is soon formed below the head by joining the legs together with a single line. A neck and other parts of the anatomy are gradually added, until there is a well-defined sketch of a human being. The proportions are still wrong, however, and it takes some time for the head, in particular, to shrink to its natural size.

While this is going on, similar developments are taking place with the portrayal of houses, animals and flowers. Eventually, between the ages of six and twelve, these innocent, universal images are obliterated by educational influences. The young artists are trained by adults who impose upon them the traditions of their particular society. The children are told to 'do it this way' or 'do it that way', when forming a picture. By the time their hands are capable of placing lines on a flat surface with precision, they are already showing strong cultural bias.

When they reach the teenage phase, most modern children will, sadly, have lost interest in picture-making. This is largely because they are now required to undertake the extremely difficult task of mastering accurate representation of the external world. What would happen if they were allowed to follow their own dictates and continue to play with visual shapes without adult interference is a tantalizing question that cannot be answered. In modern education the adult view of art training is that it should always begin with the conquest of the recording function of picture-making. This has the effect of deterring all but a tiny percentage of young people and reducing art to a fringe subject. In other cultures, at other times, where the symbolic or decorative functions of art have been considered more significant, almost all young people have retained an interest in creative art and the culture has benefited as a result.

In Western society the recording function of art reached its peak in the last few centuries, when representational art was considered to be the only art. Native and tribal arts were considered barbaric and worthless. The passion for accuracy became so intense that eventually, in the Victorian epoch, photography was invented. This rapidly improved to the point where it took over almost all the recording duties previously performed by artists. Still photography grew into moving photography and eventually to video-recording. For historical record, the television screen replaced the art gallery.

The world of fine art responded in an intriguing way to this change. At first there was an attempt to rival the new techniques. The Impressionists attempted to catch a 'fleeting impression' of a scene, in competition with the camera. This was soon abandoned and, instead of competing, the art world set about a gradual return to its more playful roots.

The Cubists began to split up their images, returning to the angular shapes seen on many tribal works of art. They were followed by artists such as Klee, Miró and Dubuffet

Before the advent of photography, art bore the heavy burden of recording the visual world. The result was the development of immense technical skill, but usually at the expense of playful creativity.

The invention of photography had a major impact on the visual arts. Initially, the reaction of the Impressionists was to rival the camera by capturing fleeting moments (*below*), but from that point onwards artists became increasingly experimental, gradually returning art to its playful roots.

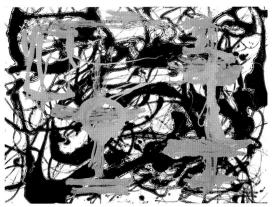

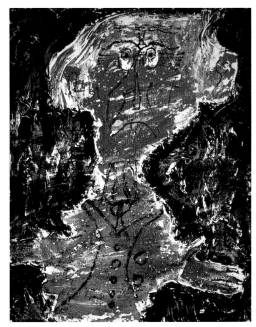

The Cubists started to dissect the visual world (*top right*), then imagery became increasingly primitive (*left*), until at last painting reached the stage of joyously free pattern-making (*above*). Works by Monet (*top left*), Braques (*top right*), Dubuffet (*left*), and Pollock (*above*).

who took their imagery back to a more childlike condition. Later still, the abstractions of Mondrian and Nicholson were back to the very early diagram stage. And finally, with the organic abstractions of Pollock and the Tachistes, the infantile scribble stage had returned.

In other words, following the invention of photography and the removal of the recording function of art, the aesthetic process went into reverse, the world of fine art returning, step by step, to the purely inventive, playful expression seen in young children. In doing so, however, it did not, as some traditionalists would have us believe, become childish. There is a world of difference between the childish and the childlike. The playfulness of modern art is executed with a mature, sophisticated approach that puts it on a par with any other phase in art history. It makes it less accessible to those who have become entrenched in the 'art as record' philosophy but for all others it is once again joyously free of restraints and formal duties.

In order to gain further insights into the primary stages of artistic development, it was necessary to find a source of painted material that was extremely simple and yet was fashioned by strong, muscular hands which put each line precisely where the artist wanted it to go. For this it was necessary to turn away from human artists and look instead at the work of our closest living relative, the chimpanzee.

It was back in the 1950s that I began a serious study of ape picture-making. I knew that a few chimpanzees had been persuaded to make simple drawings, both in Russia and the United States, and I was keen to take that pioneering work much further. I acquired a young male chimpanzee, called 'Congo', and started offering him drawing materials. Once he had mastered the art of drawing, I switched him to painting, giving him the exciting new element of bright colours. Over a period of three years he produced nearly four hundred pictures and, with them, I was able to get much closer to the origins of human art than by any other means.

Interestingly, his favourite colour was red – echoing the preference of the very earliest of human artists. And there were many other similarities. When offered a white card he would make lines on it that showed a primitive level of composition. The position of each line he made had an influence on the position of the line that would follow it. In other words, he did not make random scribbles but a distinct pattern.

This pattern usually filled the space available but did not go beyond it. In other words, the chimpanzee, like a human artist worked within the space available. As the weeks passed, certain patterns occurred again and again, and these were varied slightly with each expression.

For example, the most popular type of chimpanzee drawing or painting consisted of a fan-shaped pattern – a group of radiating lines coming closer together at the bottom of the page. More than ninety of Congo's pictures (roughly twenty-four per cent) included this fan pattern element. They appeared over a two-year period and could fairly be described as the animal's 'dominant theme'. This theme was varied in a number of ways: 1 simple fan; 2 fan with curved base; 3 stippled fan; 4 split fan; 5 split fan with central spot; 6 main fan with subsidiary fan; 7 twisted fan; 8 lopsided fan; 9 reversed fan.

The inspiration for the first fan pattern appeared to arise from the actions of bed-making. When a young chimpanzee in the wild makes its bed for the night, it does so by drawing stems and leaves towards itself. When Congo drew a fan pattern, he made the lines 'come towards him', as if he was trying to gather them in. Once he had mastered the fan pattern, however, this influence waned. The fan became a 'concept' in the ape's mind. This is proved by the many ways in which he tried to vary the simple, original shape.

At one stage he became obsessed with splitting his fan pattern into two parts, left and right, with a gap in the middle. Then, in several pictures, he enjoyed filling in this gap with a blob of paint. This central spot gave the picture an attractive sense of balance and composition. At another time he painted a large central fan and then added to it a smaller, subsidiary fan in the right-hand corner of the picture. But perhaps the most fascinating of all his fan patterns was the one that he made by reversing his hand actions. Instead of starting each line at the top of the page and drawing them down towards his body, he started at the bottom of the page and drew the lines upwards and outwards. This caused him considerable difficulty and he concentrated on the drawing more intensely than ever before.

After the long period dominated by various fan patterns, he eventually discovered the delights of making circular shapes. These usually led to wildly repeated circling actions of the hand and frequently to complete 'blot-outs' of the page. On one memorable occasion, however, he did make a good, central circle and then add details inside it. In young humans

These three paintings were produced by 'Congo' the chimpanzee. They reveal that an ape brain is capable of making simple aesthetic judgements. They demonstrate compositional control and thematic variation. Without training, the patterns he made were well balanced and scaled to fill the space available. They also showed the development of a theme – a fan-shaped pattern – which he then varied by splitting it in two, adding a central spot, or curving the base.

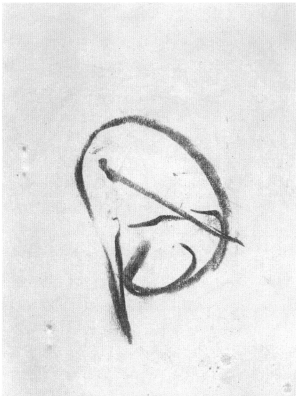

*Although the chimpanzee Congo made several hundred pictures, he never reached the stage of creating a pictorial image. With this drawing he almost managed it, forming a circle and then placing marks inside it. For the human child, this is the precursor of its first image – a face. Three million years ago, our ape-men ancestors had seen a face in the Makapansgat Pebble, but the modern chimpanzee failed to make this connection.*

this 'marked circle' was the precursor of the act of portraying the face, with eyes, nose and mouth inside a circular head. In the chimpanzee this threshold was never passed.

All this adds up to the fact that the chimpanzee brain is capable of making simple 'scribble' pictures in which there is the control of composition, the filling of available space, the creation of visual themes and the running of variations on these themes. The ape paintings were done without any training or reward. No food prizes were given. In fact the animal became so intent on the production of his pictures that any attempt to stop him before he considered that he had finished would result in a screaming temper tantrum. Although the pictures appeared to be no more than primitive scribbles and daubs to most of the humans who saw them, to the animal himself their creation was of the utmost importance.

Given these similarities with human art, what were the differences? First and foremost, the ape never managed to reach the stage of pictorial representation. He is simply a pattern-maker. He went on, year after year, producing abstract shapes but never combined these into complex units. The nearest he came to a pictorial image was the marked circle and that was an exceptional, isolated case.

Secondly, the ape was never interested in his work after it had been completed. He was an 'action painter', intrigued only by the performance of creating the picture. Once it was complete he was finished with it. Third, he always needed help in setting up the 'studio'. Apes in the wild do not spontaneously produce scribbles or works of art.

Nevertheless, the animal's ability must not be underestimated. Small children also require assistance to start painting. Like the ape, they must be given the sheets of paper and suitable painting materials. They also show little interest in their finished works. Again, like the ape, they are action painters. It is usually only their teachers or parents who admire the finished works, preserve them and encourage comments on them.

Undoubtedly, the most significant feature of the ape art was its demonstration of 'thematic variation'. The fact that this could occur at the level of the chimpanzee brain means that it is a fundamental part of the aesthetic process. It leads to another of the basic features of human art, namely classification.

Consider the nature of childhood games. A new game is invented. This is the creative phase, when innovation occurs. The high level of curiosity of our species leads us, again and again, to try out something new. We explore and experiment until we find something novel that appeals to us. This is the moment of originality, the time of rebellion and risk-taking.

Having settled on a new game, we play it over and over. Soon we are bored and so we start to vary it a little, then a little more. Eventually we exhaust it and start searching for some other, novel theme, to repeat the process all over again.

This is the way children play and it is the way that the chimpanzee paints. But with humans a new stage may be reached. If the game is a good one, with great potential for skill, beauty and entertainment, we give it a name and start to introduce vague rules to control it. Eventually we formalize it and make those rules rigid. Now the playful nature of the game is almost submerged beneath ritual procedures. Our simple childhood game has become a professional adult sport.

If these play rules are transferred from the world of sport to the world of art, we find ourselves in the world of the 'art expert', the 'genre' and the 'specialized category'. Once a type of art has been labelled and categorized, it is possible to rate all works of art that fall into that category in terms of their quality and value. Whether it be Surrealist paintings, antique snuff-boxes, Indian miniatures or Japanese armour, once a category exists it can be hardened into a distinct class of art objects and immediately surrounded by connoisseurs, dealers, critics, authorities, auctioneers and valuations.

Now a new game is played, called taxophilia – the love of classification. It no longer has anything to do with the creation of these objects, indeed, it is best if they are no longer being created, so that the category is complete and finite. It has instead to do with that elusive quality, beauty. Each object within a particular category is classified according to its type and beauty, and valued accordingly. Immensely elaborate and largely spurious aesthetic principles are established to deal with this difficult problem. They are argued over interminably by scholars around the world, who try desperately to establish rules of good taste and bad taste in every genre but who find that these keep crumbling between their fingers.

This is a delightfully subtle game that cloaks itself in immense solemnity. The catch is that nobody quite understands what beauty is. It remains the last great mystery of science. It is very real but also very elusive. It gives exquisite pleasure to those who are attuned to it, in any particular category of art, and totally bewilders those who are not. One only has to visit a tribal ceremony in some obscure culture to realize how subtle it is. The colourful costume that seems so splendid to us may be the lowest, crudest, most unattractive of all

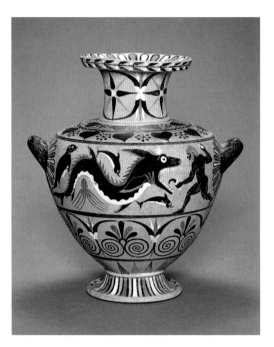 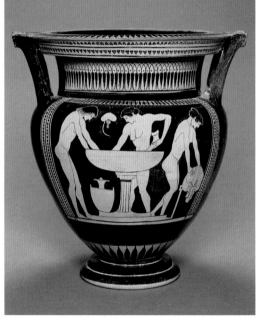

those present as far as the local participants are concerned. Until we learn the subtle rules of that particular style of art, we will be lost. And there is hardly an art form in the world that does not require some kind of connoisseurship before it can be fully appreciated, when playing the taxophilic game.

Because works of art become classified and graded in this way, it follows that they are considered to have a particular value in each case. This can set up intense competition between 'art lovers' and collectors all over the globe. Great art collections and museums vie with one another for the best available examples and vast sums are paid for works of art that once could have been bought for next to nothing. This is the subsidiary function of art as treasure.

Related to treasure is the concept of skill. Much of the pleasure of art lies in the skill with which it is made. Expertise is greatly admired. It involves a great expenditure of labour, either in the learning process or in the final execution, or both. In other words, one feature of art is that it should be a display of human ability for ability's sake. It involves talent, rising from that of apprentice to the level of genius.

*Taxophilia is the love of classifying things. Once we have established a style of art we begin playing the game of arguing over which examples are the best. Sometimes this is settled in a practical way at auction. These two Greek vases were recently sold at Sotheby's and one fetched thirty-three times as much as the other. For those who are not connoisseurs of Greek art it is difficult to decide which is the more valuable one. (The answer is on page 213.)*

The principles of adult play are applied not only to art but also to almost all other aspects of human endeavour. The great chef converts the simple act of eating into an elaborate sensory experience. In the world of high fashion, the simple demands of comfort and modesty in clothing are almost completely overshadowed by matters of style and taste. The same is true of house furnishings and decoration. Even the highly practical world of architecture is not free from human playfulness. From the ornate capitals of ancient columns to the wild excesses of Disneyland castles, the game is played wherever the architect can persuade his clients to allow him to go beyond the needs of simple security and comfort.

We play sex games, called dancing. We play war games and hunting games, called sport. We play travel games, called tourism – when we visit places we have no need to visit but where curiosity demands that we poke our noses, if only for a few tantalizing weeks.

As soon as our basic needs are satisfied, as soon as we have gone 'beyond survival', we are off and running. The naked ape should really be rechristened the creative ape. At our best we remain, all our lives, childlike adults, ready at the slightest excuse to indulge in mature play. If ever we give this up and become depressingly earnest, pious adult-adults, we will have betrayed our great biological heritage as the most exuberant, most mischievously imaginative animal on this planet. When that happens, if ever it does, it will be time for us to move on and make way for some more attractive species to replace us. In the meantime the beautiful game of life is ours for the taking.

There may be those who feel that by calling man's greatest achievements 'adult play', I am belittling them. But I am not. My point is that we have never taken play seriously

Human playfulness invades most aspects of modern life, even the intensely functional and practical world of architecture: the Best Store in Sacramento and the controversial Headington Shark.

*Even the solemn business of warfare is relived as an elaborate game; and the boring traffic-jammed world of modern transportation is enlivened by outbursts of adult playfulness.*

211

enough. To many people, our greatest achievement is to be found in the realms of such pursuits as commerce, technology, medicine, politics and economics. But to me these are merely means to one of two ends: either better human survival or better adult play. If successful commerce is concerned with, for example, food and drink, then it is either helping to satisfy hunger and thirst or it is helping to improve the subtle aesthetics of gastronomic play.

If modern technology brings us the benefits of more advanced creature comforts, we are extremely grateful but we do not sit around marvelling at the inner workings of our air-conditioning units or our refrigerators, our radios or our telephones. We simply use them as a means to many other ends. If medicine is concerned with curing diseases, that is not an end in itself but a means to a healthier life – to survive better or to enjoy adult play better.

The essential dream of modern politics and economics is to ensure personal freedoms and affluence for all. The unspoken concept behind this endeavour is to take the world's population 'beyond survival' and into the realms of advanced, mature, adult play.

Our greatest, most supremely human quality is our insatiable curiosity. We have gone from mud hut to moon rocket in just a few thousand years – a mere blink of the eye in evolutionary time. In the process we have transformed the face of the earth and built structures so impressive and so vast that some of them are visible from the moon to which we have travelled. We have done this because we have never stopped asking questions and, once we have found the answers, have used these to help us to ask even more.

Of all the many millions of animal species that have ever lived on this small planet we, the human animal, are by far the most extraordinary. But why us? Why have we gone so far when other close relatives, such as the gorilla and the chimpanzee, are left skulking in remote tropical forests? What is so special about our story that has enabled us effectively to rule the world?

*For some, the collecting of art objects as precious treasures detracts from their greatest significance – as creative events. By deliberately employing ephemeral materials, it is possible to focus attention on the making of the art rather than the keeping of it, as here with the world's largest sandcastle on a beach in Holland.*

*Greek vases on page 208: the one on the left was sold for £2 201 500 and the one on the right for £65 300.*

In a nutshell, it is because we were primates that stood up and became cooperative hunters. The fact that we were primates meant that we had a good brain and an unspecialized body, capable of many kinds of action. If we had possessed a smaller brain or a more specialized body we would have been unable to take the next step. That step was upward. By rearing up we (literally) gained a free hand to exploit the environment. We were able to make tools and use them intelligently. We were then able to kill prey.

Hunting made us braver, less selfish, more cooperative (out of necessity, not morality), more able to concentrate on long-term goals and, above all, better fed. The new high-protein diet enabled us to become even more intelligent. Our urge to hunt cooperatively gave us the need to become more communicative. We developed language and, with it, an understanding of complex symbolism. With this symbolism we were able to replace ancient actions with modern equivalents. We could make one thing stand for another so convincingly that we were able to take the make-believe world of children's play and develop our body language into acting, athletics and ballet; our hunting into sport, gambling, exploration and collecting; our speech into singing, poetry and theatre; and our cooperation into altruism and generosity. We were the magic combination, the threshold leaper, the risk-taker, the venerable child for all occasions.

With their often stunningly beautiful bodies, other animals are remarkable for what they are. We, with our puny, rather unimpressive bodies, are remarkable for what we have done. And what we will undeniably do in the future, for the story has hardly begun ...

*Three hundred and sixty miles above the earth two astronauts repair the £1.3 billion Hubble telescope, enabling us to see stars ten billion light years away and perhaps discover the size of the universe. Our inquisitiveness – our mature playfulness – knows no bounds. Curiosity may have killed the cat, but it has been the making of mankind.*

# *Acknowledgements*

This book has been written to accompany the six-part television series made by the BBC's Natural History Unit in Bristol. I owe a debt of gratitude to all the members of the large team that made the programmes. Their enthusiasm for the project was unflagging and the immense care and effort they took to record the various patterns of human behaviour all over the globe was inspiring. I offer my special thanks to every one of the people listed on the opposite page.

I have to confess that, originally, I had my doubts about the possibility of making this series. The idea of reducing the whole of human behaviour to six hours of television seemed to me to be doomed to superficiality. I argued that to make a comprehensive series on human behaviour would take, not six, but six thousand hours. But my senior producer, Mike Beynon, who first proposed the idea, is not a man who allows an obstacle to stand in the way of his television dreams. When he senses an exciting television goal, he becomes – in the best human tradition – a symbolic hunter. Faced with my reservations, he devised a new strategy. Instead of making the series about the whole of human behaviour, we would limit it to those aspects I had written about in my books. These books covered a wide range, it was true, but they did at least favour certain subjects and we would do the same in the programmes.

It was agreed that we would base the first programme on my book *Manwatching*, the second on *The Naked Ape*, the third on *The Human Zoo*, the fourth on *Intimate Behaviour*, the fifth on *Babywatching* and *The Book of Ages*, and the sixth on *The Biology of Art*. These books each had a main topic. Respectively: body language, the evolution of our species, urbanization, intimacy, the human life cycle, and art. Each of these topics in turn related to a basic, underlying aspect of human behaviour, namely: communication, feeding, territory, sex, rearing, and play. By making these six biological imperatives of the human animal the central themes of our six programmes it was possible to place the project squarely inside the frame of reference of the Natural History Unit of the BBC, rather than in some other department. Also, by making it more personal, more closely related to my past studies of the human species, it was possible to avoid the all-embracing superficiality that I had feared might overtake us.

My debt to Mike Beynon, who initiated the whole project, is huge. And I would also like to single out for special praise the production teams with whom I travelled the world: producers Graham Booth, Clive Bromhall, John Macnish and Martin Weitz; chief cameraman Eric Huyton, researchers Vanessa Berlowitz and Penny Smith; and production assistants Liz Stevens and Di Williams. They were, without exception, a joy to work with, as were all the various camera operators and sound technicians, who had to put up with many trying circumstances and sometimes a degree of danger. For the picture research on this book I am especially grateful for the expert endeavours of Jennifer Fry, and for their editorial expertise, Sheila Ableman and Nicky Copeland of BBC Books.

Finally, an additional word of thanks to all those who assisted the television production team with expert advice on special subjects: Dr Peter Andrews, Molly Badham, Dr Paul Bahn, Dr Robin Baker, Carol Beckwith, Dr Nelly Bedrova, Dr Mark Bellis, Ino Bonello, Anthony Borbon, Richard Brereton, Christopher Dean, Dr Ellen Dissanayake, Lesley Downer, Robin Dunbar, David Gibbs, Jenny Hall, Anne Hawley, Ken Hedges, Diana James, Mark Johnston, Jenny Kaye, Sheila Kitzinger, Dr Giannis Kugiumutzakis, Chris Lyons, Dr Neil Marlow, Michael O'Hanlan, Dr Richard Rayner, Peter Rich, Dr Vernon Reynolds, David Roxborough, Tammy

Roxborough, Dr Tim Sanders, Sue Savage-Rumbaugh, Chloe Sayer, Wendy Stephenson, Dr Chris Stringer, Professor Colwyn Trevarthen, Dr Walter Van Beek, Londa Van Elsacker, Kristel de Vleeschouwer, Dr Marsden Wagner, Kaly Walker and Leon Yost.

TELEVISION PRODUCTION TEAM

*Series Producer*
MIKE BEYNON

*Producer*
MARTIN WEITZ

*Assistant Producers*
GRAHAM BOOTH
CLIVE BROMHALL
JOHN MACNISH

*Production Co-ordinators*
LIZ STEVENS
DI WILLIAMS

*Production Secretaries*
MELISSA BLANDFORD
LOUISE DAWE-LANE

*Unit Manager*
NICKY SPODE

*Series Researchers*
VANESSA BERLOWITZ
PENNY SMITH

*Graphic Designers*
PAUL BOND
4:2:2 VIDEOGRAPHICS

*Video Editors*
TIM COOPE
ALAN HOIDA
ANDY MORT
CHRISTINE SCULFOR

*Sound Recordists*
ALAN BARKER
JOHN DUMONT
KEVIN MEREDITH
JOHN RODDA
JEFF WOOD
BILL WREN

*Camera Operators*
ALI ABAD
TONY ALLEN
MIKE BOLAND
DEREK BROMHALL
NEIL BROMHALL
ROB BROWNHILL
JOEY FORSYTE
RICHARD GANNICLIFT
JEFF GOODMAN
RAWN D. HAIRSTON
ALAN HEYWARD
ERIC HUYTON
MIKE LEMMON
BILL MEGALOS

MARK MOLESWORTH
PATRICK MORRISON
PATTI MUSICARO
JEREMY POLLARD
RICK PRICE
RAHUL RANAVIVE
SASKIA VAN REES
MIZOSLAV ROUSSIMOV
SUSANNAH SHAW
CLAUDIO TONDI
KEITH TURNER
RICHARD VARNER
JOHN WATERS
MARIANNE WILDING
ALECOS YIANNAROS
AMY BOWER
CIAN DE BUITLEAR
PAUL CHEARY
JOHN COUZENS
TINA DIFELICIANTONIO
RAY GIBBONS
DOUG HARTINGTON
MIKE HUGHES
BELINDA PARSONS
MARK PAYNE-GILL
ELMER POSTLE
ROBIN RISELY
TOM RUSSELL
DAVID SCOTT

# Further Books by Desmond Morris

Books by Desmond Morris dealing with various aspects of human behaviour are as follows:

1962   THE BIOLOGY OF ART. Methuen, London.

1965   MEN AND SNAKES. (with Ramona Morris) Hutchinson, London.

1966   MEN AND APES. (with Ramona Morris) Hutchinson, London.

1966   MEN AND PANDAS. (with Ramona Morris) Hutchinson, London.

1967   PRIMATE ETHOLOGY. (editor) Weidenfeld and Nicolson, London.

1967   THE NAKED APE. Jonathan Cape, London.

1969   THE HUMAN ZOO. Jonathan Cape, London.

1971   INTIMATE BEHAVIOUR. Jonathan Cape, London.

1977   MANWATCHING: A FIELD-GUIDE TO HUMAN BEHAVIOUR. Jonathan Cape, London.

1979   GESTURES: THEIR ORIGINS AND DISTRIBUTION. (with Peter Collett, Peter Marsh and Marie O'Shaughnessy) Jonathan Cape, London.

1981   THE SOCCER TRIBE. Jonathan Cape, London.

1983   THE BOOK OF AGES. Jonathan Cape, London.

1985   THE ART OF ANCIENT CYPRUS. Phaidon, Oxford.

1985   BODYWATCHING: A FIELD-GUIDE TO THE HUMAN SPECIES. Jonathan Cape, London.

1988   THE HUMAN NESTBUILDERS. Crown, Darwen.

1990   THE ANIMAL CONTRACT. Virgin Books, London.

1991   BABYWATCHING. Jonathan Cape, London.

1992   CHRISTMAS WATCHING. Jonathan Cape, London.

1994   THE HUMAN ANIMAL. BBC Books, London.

# *Index*

fossils, 49, 61
France, *29*, 30, 42, 194, 195
freezing, cryonics, *180*, 181–2
fruit, 64–5
fur, 53, 57, 157

gambling, 69, 108
games, 69, 108, 188, 206–7, 209
gangs, 99–103, *100–1*, 119
gates, 99
Gaudi, Antonio, *110*, 111
geese, 135
gender signals, *120–1*, 122–7, *126*
genes: and ageing, 179–81
    genetic engineering, 179–81
    grandparents, 175
    homosexuality, 150
    immortality, 156, 183
    non-breeding individuals, 156
    sexuality and, 138, 139
    shared with chimpanzee, 6–7
genitals: concealment, 124
    fig sign, 26–7
    mutilation, 145
    sexual arousal, 133–4
geometry, 194
gestures, 12–16, *14–15*, 23–31, *24–5*,
    *29*, 36, 99–102
gibbons, 10
giraffes, 70
goats, 93
Golan Heights, 188
gorillas, 60, 213
    feeding, 70
    genes, 7
    penis, 133
graffiti, *100*, 102, 111–14
Grand Seraglio, 140–1
grandparents, 175–6, *177*
Greece, 22, *25*, 26, *208*
groups, synchrony, 33

Hagerhai tribe, *51*
hair, 53
    gender signals, 127
    hair-tracts, 56, 57
    protection of head from sun, 12
    pubic, 125
hallways, 95, 98
hands: courtship, 130–1
    development of, 12
    gestures, 12–16, *14–15*, 23–31,
        *24–5*, *29*, 36, 99–102
    hand shrug, 37
    kissing, 22

pointing, 17
    webbing, 57
Hardy, Sir Alister, 56–7
harems, 139–41, *140*
Hawaii, 28, *29*
head: courtship, 131
    nodding, 22
    shaking, 22
    shape of baby's, 166–8, *167*
    tossing, 22
    *see also* face
Headington Shark, *210*
heat, cooling the body, 12
Henry V, King, 23
herbivores, 52, 63, 65, 70
hierarchy, social, 103–4
hieroglyphs, 189–90, *190*
hitch-hiking, 30–1
hobbies, 68, 108
homes, 63–4, 82, 92–5
homosexuals, 150–1, 156
hormones, sex, 116, 126
hospitals, childbirth, 160–1, 162
houses, 95–9
Hubble telescope, *215*
humour, sense of, 183
Hundertwasser House, Vienna, *110*,
    111
hunting, 49–53, *50–1*, 61, 63
    carrying prey home, 10
    cave paintings, 195–7
    cooling the body, 12
    cooperation, 52, 63, 214
    and development of intelligence,
        52–3, 184, 214
    substitutes for, *66–7*, 68–70, 77–81,
        *79*
hunting dogs, 61, 62
huts, 92–4, *96–7*
hygiene, 63–4

immortality, 179–81, 183
immune system, 115
Impressionism, 199, *201*
infections, 115
influenza epidemics, 115
Innuit, *51*
insulting gestures, 23–7, *24–5*
intelligence:
    and adult play, 184
    development of, 63, 64
    language and, 176–8
Italy, 22–3, 30, 42
itching, 36–7
Izumi, Shigechiyo, 183

Jackson, Michael, 104
Japan, 27, *29*, 30, 43
jealousy, sexual, 139
jewellery, 105
jungles, 82–4

Kenya, *58*, *192*
Khirokitia, 93–4
kissing, 21–2, *128*, 130
kitchens, 95, 98
Klee, Paul, 199–202
knowledge, tribal elders, 176
Kyoto, 27

labour, 157–62
language: breath control and, 60
    and cultural separation, 46–7
    development of, 52, 64, 171, 172,
        176–8, 214
    verbal abuse, 77–80
    written, 189–90
Lascaux, 195
lawlessness, 103
leaders, 103–4, *106*
'leakage', non-verbal, 36–8
learning, 172, 176
legs, skirt lengths, 124
leisure activities, 68
lemmings, 115
Liberace, 104
life-span, 175–6, 182–3
Limeworks Quarry, Transvaal, 186–7
lions, 184, *185*
lips, 20–2, 124–5, 133
living rooms, 95, 98
loners, 33
longevity, 182–3
Lorenz, Konrad, 135
Los Angeles, 99–103, *100–1*, 111
loyalty, 80
lying, 36–8
lynch mobs, *79*

Magritte, René, 190–1, *191*
Makapansgat Pebble, 187–8, *187*, 191,
    *205*
males: gender signals, *121*, 125, *126*
    hunting, 63, 64
    sexuality, 137–44
manners, 85–8
markers, territorial, 99, *100–1*
marriage, 118, *136*
    *see also* pair-bonding
mating *see* sexuality
meat-eating, 49–52, 63, 70, 71, *72*
Mediterranean countries, 42, 119, 154

# Index

# *Picture Credits*

BBC Books would like to thank the following for providing photographs and for permission to reproduce copyright material. While every effort has been made to trace and acknowledge all copyright holders, we would like to apologize should there have been any errors or omissions.

Key: T – top, C – centre, B – bottom, L – left, R – right, TL – top left, TR – top right, CL – centre left, CR – centre right, BL – bottom left, BR – bottom right

ALLSPORT page 58 (T, Simon Bruty); ANCIENT ART AND ARCHITECTURE COLLECTION page 27; ARCAID pages 112 (L, John Stuart Miller) and 210 (L, Richard Bryant); AUSTRIAN NATIONAL TOURIST OFFICE page 110; GRAHAM BOOTH pages 189, 192 (T) and 212; BRIDGEMAN ART LIBRARY pages 76 (Ali Meyer/Naturhistorisches Museum, Vienna), 106 (TR, *Henry VIII* by Hans Holbein/Board of Trustees of the National Museums and Galleries on Merseyside/Walker Art Gallery, Liverpool), 140 (*Harem*, c. 1850, by John Frederick Lewis/Victoria and Albert Museum, London), 191 (*Ceci n'est pas une pipe* by René Magritte/ Giraudon/ Los Angeles County Museum of Art/© A.D.A.G.P., Paris, and D.A.C.S., London, 1994), 200 (detail of *Fruit and Flowers* by Isaac Soreau/Musée du Petit Palais, Paris) and 201 (TL, *Boulevard des Capucines* by Claude Monet/ Pushkin Museum, Moscow; TR, *Violin and Glass* by Georges Braque, © A.D.A.G.P., Paris, and D.A.C.S., London, 1994; BL, *Magician with Red Skin* by Jean Dubuffet, © A.D.A.G.P., Paris, and D.A.C.S., London, 1994; BR, *Yellow, Grey, Black*, 1948, by Jackson Pollock/© 1994, Pollock-Krasner Foundation/A.R.S., N.Y.); CLIVE BROMHALL pages 18 (TL), 39, 136 (B), 146 and 152 (C); FRED BRUEMMER page 51 (R); BUBBLES page 72 (T); BRUCE COLEMAN pages 11 (inset), 18 (BL, John Cancalosi), 167 (TR, Rod Williams) and 170 (TR, Christer Fredriksson); MARY EVANS PICTURE LIBRARY pages 79 (B) and 149 (BR); WERNER FORMAN ARCHIVE pages 158 (TL, Peabody Museum, Harvard University) and 180 (TL); FLPA pages 90 (T. Whittaker) and 185 (TL, E. and D. Hosking); SALLY AND RICHARD GREENHILL pages 83, 91 and 159 (B); ROBERT HARDING PICTURE LIBRARY pages 11 (Bildagentur Schuster/Alexandre), 18 (TR, Explorer/Fievet), 67 (T, Bildagentur Schuster/Bramaz), 86 (T, Adam Woolfitt), 96 (B, F. Jackson), 96–7, 109, 113 (R, M. Jenner), 121 (TR), 136 (T, Paul Freestone), 149 (BL), 159 (T), 177 (Adam Woolfitt), 180 (TR), 185 (BL), 192 (C, Paul van Riel), 192–3 (Arthus Bertrand), 210 (R, Walter Rawlings) and 211 (TR, Rob Cousins; BR, S. H. and D. H. Cavanaugh); MICHAEL HOLFORD page 196; HORIZON page 167 (BL, Heidi Ecker); HULTON-DEUTSCH pages 24 (C), 126, 127 and 158 (BR); ERIC HUYTON back cover; IMAGE BANK page 24 (B, Werner Bokelberg); IMAGES pages 72–3 and 167 (TL); ISRAEL ANTIQUITIES AUTHORITY/ISRAEL MUSEUM page 188; JESSICA JOHNSON page 55 (inset); KATZ pages 15 (TL, Richard Baker; BL, Ron Haviv/Saba) and 180 (BL, Machete); ANDREW LAWSON page 29 (BR); LONDON FEATURES INTERNATIONAL page 24 (T); MAGNUM pages 29 (TR, S. McCurry), 66 (CR, Dennis Stock), 83 (B, Michael K. Nichols), 86 (B, Scianna) and 106–7 (René Burri); JOHN MACNISH page 100–1; MINDEN PICTURES page 72 (B, Jim Brandenburg); DESMOND MORRIS pages 25, 58 (B), 204 (TL, Michael Lyster; TR and B, Alan Clifton) and 205 (T, Alan Clifton); MUSÉE DE L'HOMME, PARIS page 158 (BL); NASA page 215; NETWORK pages 18 (BR, Justin Leighton) and 192 (CL, Mike Goldwater); NHPA page 185 (BR, John Shaw); OXFORD SCIENTIFIC FILMS page 72 (C, Steve Turner); PACIFIC STOCK page 29 (L, Bachmann); PETIT FORMAT page 170 (BR, J. P. Casaubon); PHOTO RESEARCHERS pages 87 (inset, Bobbie Kingsley) and 112–13 (Joseph Nettis); PLANET EARTH PICTURES pages 19 (inset, Brian Kenney), 50–1 (John Downer) and 54–5 (D. Perrine); REFLECTIONS (Jennie Woodcock) pages 128 (L and R inset) and 170 (L and CR); REX FEATURES pages 14 (TL, Sipa/Larry Reider; TR, Peter Heimsath; BL, Peter Brooker; BR, *The Times*), 15 (TR, Peter Brooker; BR, Patsy Lynch), 34–5 (*Today*), 44, 45 (TL), 66 (B, *Today*), 66–7 (Sipa/Cole), 74 (T, Sipa/Frilet), 78–9 (Ian Black), 106 (L, Sipa/T. B. Gibod; BR), 107 (R, Nils Jorgensen), 129 (BR, Robert Fergus), 149 (T) and 180 (BR, Sipa/Alcor); SOTHEBY'S page 208; TONY STONE WORLDWIDE pages 86–7 (Ed Pritchard) and 110 (T, David Hanson); SYNDICATION INTERNATIONAL page 45 (R); UNIVERSITY OF WITWATERSRAND, JOHANNESBURG (Bernard Price Institute for Palaeontological Research) page 187; MARTIN WEITZ page 164–5; ZEFA front cover and pages 1, 2–3, 19 (Havlicek), 35, 59 (Jack Fields), 66 (TL), 74 (B, Damm), 120–1, 121 (TL, Eggermont; B), 128 (R), 129 (L, TR), 152–3 (Sunak), 167 (BR, Lacz-Lemoin), 185 (TR, Norman) and 192 (BR, O. Luz).